BREAKEVEN-POINT

TALHA SARESHWALA

Contents

Preface

It has been 30 years since I started my career as a humble entrepreneur. This journey, full of excitement, experiences, rewards, and learning's, is very close to my heart because of one important reason: My unconditional faith in following ethical business practice and following it throughout in its totality. My dedication, work ethics and never-say-die attitude have largely contributed to this success as a businessman and social entrepreneur.

100% of the business of this world is run by just 7.25% of its population. Being a businessman an entrepreneur itself is like joining an elite club of visionary people making endless manufacturing and servicing possible for 92.5% people on this planet.

An Entrepreneur needs to be a visionary, who aims to be the "best in the manner in which he operates, best in the products he delivers, and best in our value system and ethics." A goal to empower and provide employees with dynamic career paths in congruence with corporate objectives. All-round potential development and performance improvement should be ensured by regular in-house and external training. The Entrepreneur from the outset should have a broad and clear vision to take the company to new heights and territory. He also needs to understood that success had to be earned and every success had to be repeated, with dedication, synergism and providing the best customer service and a constant emphasis on belief that happy employees create happy customers which will race towards success.

This book a non-fiction will be a riveting take on the world of entrepreneurship. Besides compulsive reading, it would also be a guide for aspiring and ignited minds who wish to start a business and make a difference. It would offer its readers ideas and suggestions to take baby steps in the world of business, and to stay determined and focused to grow business smartly.

That's the reason, I thought of sharing my experience as an entrepreneur through this book. A book that can act as a catalyst for young minds, while ensuring them that ethics and principles do pay in business when followed in true spirit and action. The book would also throw light on many crucial business aspects, so that it becomes useful in all senses, such as Importance of:

- Business, and its Skills
- Business strategy for Entrepreneurs
- Leadership qualities
- Ethical Business
- MSME: Understanding of MSME, and its Benefits
- Growing Business in an Interest free environment
- Importance of Corporate Governance and last but not the least
- Women Empowerment: Business Women

I would consider my endeavour worth all its efforts if it ignites just one mind and inspire it to follow ethical business practices and make our country proud.

Further With all humility, I wish that all readers contribute their perspective and experience. Your thoughts as a small note and sharing your opinions would be a big plus. The aim for this is to create a bank of diverse inputs, which further enhances the subject's relevance. I request all to spare your precious time and support the cause of igniting the young dynamic entrepreneurial minds of our young and energetic population

Credits

I always wanted to share my experiences of my 30 years of entrepreneurial journey in whatever way I could, so I did webinars and a few lectures, but will be eternally grateful **to my Late Father Mohd Yunus Sareshwala** for inspiring me and inculcating the habit of sharing and caring. And he being an avid reader, I thought of sharing my knowledge through this Book *Welcome Entrepreneur- For A Breakeven Point*

Special **thanks to my Wife and 2 daughters** for their relentless support and encouragement throughout the writing process. **My Mother** for her never ending Duas (Prayer) and her blessings. And not to forget to thank Almighty Allah as I couldn't have done anything without him. **Alhumdullilah Totally Grateful to him.**

I have taken an Unusual approach in writing this book, in which information has been sourced and compiled from Internet, social media, attending various conferences, networking and webinars along with my thoughts, ideas, experiences and writing abilities.

Research & Editorial: Talha Sareshwala

Graphics: Free images from various Internet sites, Google

I
INTRODUCTION

Importance of business and skills

"A big business starts small," as British billionaire Richard Branson famously said.

Similarly, a true entrepreneur is a doer rather than a dreamer. *"You need to sustain yourself for 1000 days in business,"* my grandfather used to say. I believe that's the key to success and it will be your BREAK-EVEN POINT.

Business and Business Life has indeed become complicated. But remember we need to stop analysing them. Just do it. Analysis is what makes it complicates, and that's the reason we are constantly unhappy and unsuccessful. Your today is the tomorrow that you worried about yesterday. You are worrying because the act of worrying has become a habit, a reason we are not happy.

One of the main reasons for our worry is that there is so much uncertainty in Business. Uncertainty is inevitable but worrying is optional, same as Pain due to uncertainty is inevitable, but suffering is optional.
Diamonds cannot be polished without friction. Gold cannot be purified without fire. Good business people go through trials. With that experience their life becomes better, not bitter. And that is called Experience
Experience is a hard teacher, though it gives the test first and the lessons afterwards.

But still we should go through such tests, and face these problems...

Problems are Purposeful Roadblocks Offering Beneficial Lessons to Enhance Mental Strength. Inner strength comes from struggle and endurance, not when you are free from problems.

Frankly in the midst of so many problems, we don't know where we are heading. But if you look outside you will not know where you are heading. Look inside. Looking outside, you dream. Looking inside, you awaken. Eyes provide sight. Heart provides insight.

Also, sometimes not succeeding fast seems to hurt more than moving in the right direction. The reason is, Success is relative, quantified by others. Satisfaction is absolute, quantified by you. Knowing the road ahead is more satisfying than knowing you rode ahead.

So, seek not to find who you are, but to determine who you want to be. Stop looking for a purpose as to why you are here. Create it. Entrepreneurship is not a process of discovery but a process of creation, your own creation.

Face your past without regret. Handle your present with confidence. Prepare for the future without fear. My advice; Just have Faith in God and in your ability.

Keep the faith and drop the fear. Entrepreneurship in itself is a mystery to solve, not a problem to resolve. It's wonderful if you know how to live with it and handle it.

Learn the little lessons life teaches you, says motivational speaker Jim Rohn

He says, over the years he has been teaching children about a simple but powerful concept — **The Ant Philosophy**

I too think every entrepreneur should study ants. They have an amazing four-part philosophy,

first part: ants never quit:

That's a good philosophy. If they're headed somewhere and you try to stop them; they'll look for another way. They'll climb over, they'll climb under, they'll climb around. They keep looking for another way. What a neat philosophy, to never quit looking for a way to get where you're supposed to go.

second, ants think winter all summer:

That's an important perspective. You can't be so naive as to think summer (Good Days) will last forever. So, ants are gathering in their winter food in the middle of summer, so that during winter (Hard Times) they live peacefully without stepping out - what a perspective. We all have to be prepared and work harder for our better future.
Why do we need that advice? Because it is important to be realistic. In the summer, you've got to think storm. You've got to think rocks as you enjoy the sand and sun. Think ahead.

third part is that ants think summer all winter.

That is so important. During the winter, ants remind themselves, "This won't last long; we'll soon be out of here." And the first warm day, the ants are out. Means always be Positive in your thoughts If it turns cold again, they'll dive back down, but then they come out the first warm day. They can't wait to get out. Similarly, our approach to every storm in our lives should be positive and a brighter hope.

And the **last part of the ant philosophy.**
How much will an ant gather during the summer to prepare for the winter? All that it possibly can. They don't have an idea of what is Good enough. So,

we should be trying as hard as we can to achieve success or Goals we've set.

What an incredible philosophy, the 'all-that you-possibly-can' philosophy.

A business is an economic activity with the main objective of making a profit as much as possible. This profit will go on to result in growth, survival, and expansion. Furthermore, the goals can be expanded as follows:

- Market standing
- Productivity
- Innovation
- Physical and financial resources

This is what a business organization strives for and accomplishes over time: to provide quality goods or services to its customers while also protecting the environment. Allah the almighty says "Business is lawful for you" (Quran, 2:275). According to Chapra (2008) the "need fulfilment" of all in a society is of utmost importance in Islamic jurisprudence. Prophet Mohammad (SAW) was himself engaged in trade and commerce before he became a prophet. He was a successful businessman. In addition to the economic objective is the human objective, which is linked to its employees and customers, as well as social objectives.

Social objectives are very important in the life of an entrepreneur. The primary concern of this objective is the production and supply of quality and standard goods and services, the adaptation of fair trade practices, contribution to society's overall welfare, and the provision of welfare amenities.

It is critical for an entrepreneur to improve his product or services, as well as provide opportunities for teams to improve their leadership skills. To achieve high levels of employee loyalty and job satisfaction among its workforce, the entrepreneur must always be on the lookout for new ways to reach out to members of the community and expand his or her customer base.

These sound ethical practices influence and contribute to employees' commitment, investor and customer satisfaction, loyalty, and confidence. It also gives the ability to build relationships with stakeholders, thus enhancing the reputation and image of a business organization.

These are **strategic objectives**, which throws light on a company's idea to fulfil its mission. These are somewhat similar to performance goals. In other words, it's a clear set of actions and goals formulated with outlines of how a business will steer its way in a particular market. Entrepreneurship is also at the core of all Islamic values because it is all about value creation. We create value for a social impact, for wealth creation, and for economic development. Entrepreneurship gives you financial empowerment, allowing you the ability to pass it along.

How to conduct business

Business ethics implies conducting business in a way that benefits society as a whole, while also serving one's own interests. Every strategic decision has moral consequences. These ethical decisions in business have implications such as a happy workforce, increased sales, lower regulatory costs, more customers, and increased goodwill. Virtually all of the world's great religions contain in their religious texts some version of the Golden Rule: **"Do unto others as you would wish them do unto you"**. In other words, we should treat others the way we would want to be treated. This is the basic ethic that guides all religions.

What I have identified as unethical practices are the ills of an unjust interest-based economic system. Let us first understand the ancient and spiritual perspectives of interest.

Usury was defined as "the practice of charging financial gains in excess of the loan's principal amount". However, the modern definition has been tweaked to look ethical and acceptable. It is now defined "as interest at a rate that is higher than the legal or socially acceptable rate".

Spiritual perspectives

Now let's dwell upon the spiritual and religious guidelines, from both ancient and modern perspectives, that dictate the business protocols...

Ancient Hinduism: In 400 BC, the Hindu lawmaker forbade the higher castes from being usurers or lenders of interest.

Modern Hinduism: By the second century AD, Manu's laws stated that "stipulated interest beyond the legal rate being against the law cannot be recovered".

Ancient Judaism: Criticism of usury in Judaism has its roots in several biblical passages, where taking interest is forbidden, discouraged, or scorned.

Modern Judaism: Jews are not permitted to charge interest to other Jews. The non-Jews, on the other hand, can be charged interest.

Ancient Christianity: In the 5th century AD, the Roman Catholic Church prohibited taking of interest. In the 8th century AD, the action of usury was proclaimed a general criminal offence. By 131,1 Pope Clement V made the ban on usury legislation in its favour null-and-void.

Modern Christianity: They are not allowed to charge high interests as per the modern definition of usury. However, charging interest at a normal rate is allowed.

Ancient Islam: Islam identified its ills and came out clearly against its prevalent use dating back to around 600 AD.

*Modern Islam:*The definition of *Sharia* compliance is changing. In fact, *Sharia*-compliant companies are allowed to have a debt of less than 33% of their market capitalization.

The *Quran* did not just stop with an injunction on interest, but encouraged business and trade in the same sentence.

The Quran says: "Allah has permitted trade and forbidden interest."

By being interest-free/debt-free the company has inbuilt advantages. Debt-free firms are low-risk investments, preferred by both amateurs and professional investors. Debt has a higher long-term cost, and a debt-free company pays a higher dividend yield and has a higher return on equity.

There are quite a few Indian companies that are debt-free or have achieved zero-debt status. The notables are HUL, ITC, Ambuja Cement, SBI Life Insurance, HDFC AMC Ltd, Castrol, Gillette India, etc.

Being debt-free eliminates all worries and side effects that debt can bring. It gives the sense of security that comes with the fact that you don't owe anyone anything. It gives a thorough peace of mind.

Also, the Quran has given glad tidings and has glorified a true businessman by saying- ``*Their doing business does not stop them from the remembrance of God.*"

In fact, there are quite a few virtues described in the Quran and the prophet saying (*hadith*) for doing business. Doing business is not compulsory in religion but if one is in that profession, then doing business in the most ethical way is a must and compulsory for a businessman.

What are the ethical practices of a true businessman: I would like to dedicate an entire chapter in my book which is indeed very close to my heart.

Corporate governance

This is the most important aspect of ethical business. In fact, the three main pillars of corporate governance are:

- Transparency
- Accountability
- Security

The combinations of these three pillars are important in running a company successfully and forming solid professional relationships among its stakeholders, which includes key managerial employees and most importantly, the shareholders.

The goal of including corporate governance in my topic is to assist entrepreneurs in creating an environment of trust, transparency, and accountability, which is required for fostering long-term investment, financial stability, and business integrity.

Women empowerment through business

In general, the perception of us, as a Muslim community, triggers off the following questions on women:

- Can women do business?
- Can they be a successful entrepreneur?

Women, who are in leadership roles or who want to position as one, often feel they come under certain scrutiny. Hence, more women tend to become entrepreneurs to exclude gender inequality in business.

I firmly believe that a woman knows where she wants to be and has plans on how to get there. She sets her own goals and finds her own way to achieve them. Khadija *(RA)*, the first wife of the Prophet Muhammad *(SAW)*, was a successful businesswoman in her own right, who controlled one of the most important caravan trade routes in the region. She is a shining example of a strong independent Muslim woman with an entrepreneurial spirit.

Family entrepreneurship

A family entrepreneurship is an enterprise involving two or more family members. Since the majority of the ownership generally lies within a family, decisions are sometimes influenced by multiple generations of people related by blood, which in turn has the ability to influence the vision of the business and the willingness to use them to pursue their goals, like any profit organization driven by wealth, and responsibility. In a family business, counterbalancing these economic priorities are family values of love, cohesion, self-esteem, and caring.

With each member in a family enterprise secure in his or her position, innovative ideas take shape quickly due to the family staff taking risks. However, there is one major reason for a family business to fail - succession planning. The lack of proper planning and poor leadership result in family conflict that leads to a loss of direction and ultimately collapse of the business.

Our country has a high number of successful family businesses. As of 2018, India stood third on the list of family businesses with 111 companies. While these family-run businesses account for 85% of all Indian companies, they also account for the vast majority of national output and employment. However, we also have a large number of family-owned businesses in the Micro, Small & Medium Enterprise (MSME) segment.

MICRO SMALL & MEDIUM ENTERPRISE (MSME)

As we already know MSME stands for the micro, small and medium enterprises. It was introduced by the Government of India (GOI) in agreement with the Micro Small Medium Enterprises Development Act of 2006. As per this Act, MSMEs are enterprises involved in the production, processing, and preservation of goods and commodities. Recently, the GOI redefined MSMEs in terms of their level of investment and turnover, so that more and more companies can avail of maximum benefits from the government schemes, subsidies, and SOPs. MSMEs are the backbone of any developing economy and it covers only the manufacturing and service industries. Currently, the total registered MSMEs are 51 million. Registering the enterprise as MSME is optional, but a registered one gets lots of benefits from government schemes like bank loans (collateral free) subsidy on patent registration, industrial promotion subsidy, protection against delayed payments, etc.

In this book, I have tried to cover major aspects of MSME in terms of understanding its challenges, its benefits, and how to grow the business. I have also tried to incorporate major links for MSME, and Frequently Asked Questions in Appendix section to enable readers to take maximum benefit out of them.

II
BUSINESS ENTREPRENEURS IN THE MAKING

*कमाई की परिभाषा सिर्फ़ धन से तय नहीं होती, *
इसमें
तजुर्बा, रिश्ते, सम्मान और सबक...
सब कमाई के ही रूप हैं...!!

Translation: *The definition of earnings does not end at just acquisition of wealth; it includes experience, respect and learnings. All these are different forms of earnings.*

What business advice can be given to new startups, particularly entrepreneurs? *'Plan Your Work And Work Your Plan'* - this one-liner is a ticket to a lifetime of peace and prosperity.

So, go ahead and plan your work and work your plan and you'll be far more successful if you maintain a healthy work-life balance. Set out without fear and with a BIG SMILE!

Set High Goals That Are Achievable

Every human being has a goal in life and finds a purpose to fulfil that goal. No goal can be achieved without that purpose. If there is only one purpose, the goal is not fulfilled. The goal must be achievable. They should be well-defined, clear, unambiguous, and measurable with specific criteria that measure your progress toward achieving them. They must be relevant to your life purpose.

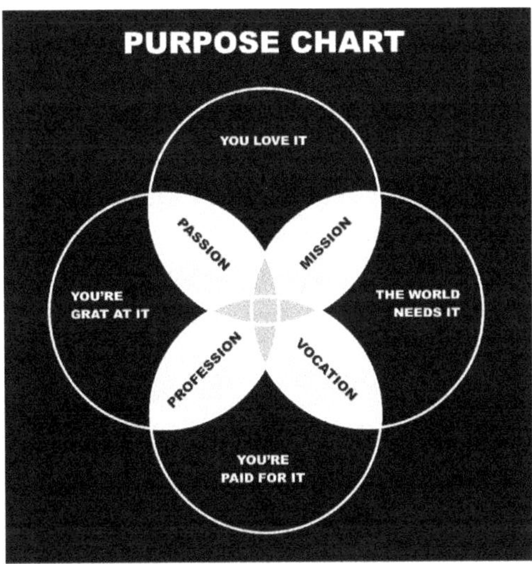

(Source: Internet)

To be successful, your goal must also be realistic and attainable. In other words, it should broaden your skills and still be a possibility. When you set an attainable goal, you may be able to identify previously overlooked opportunities or resources that can bring you closer to your goals.

Business skills are a foundation for success in the business world and include soft skills like negotiation, communication, along with analytical and organizational skills that help a business succeed. Critical thinking, and trainability are other examples of business skills. If you are a business owner, these skills equip you with the ability to meet the needs of both your consumers and employees. In business, you don't get what you deserve, you get what you negotiate. This art of negotiation is perhaps what most deeply distinguishes man from animals said Harry Martinson. According to Robert

Estabrook. He who has learned to disagree without being disagreeable has discovered the most valuable secret of a diplomat. At its core, negotiation is nothing more than communication with results. To get what you want out of life, you need to get what you want from others. While there is no magic formula for beings a successful entrepreneur, those who do succeed tend to have mastered the following set of skills: good and effective communication; being able to sell both themselves and their idea or product; strong focus; eagerness to learn and be flexible; and a solid business plan. To improve business skills, take some time to read up on the most valuable business skills needed in your industry. ... and find a mentor. Having a mentor who has extensive business experience can provide you with the guidance you may need to develop professionally. ...

Along with business Skills, Professional skills are equally important which is career competencies and abilities used in the workplace that are beneficial for nearly any job. Professional skills are a combination of both hard skills (job-specific duties that can be trained) and soft skills (transferable traits like work ethic, communication, and leadership).

Our lives improve only when we take chances, and the first and most difficult risk we can take is to be honest with ourselves.

Stephen Covey once said, "Stop setting goals. Unless you have a specific plan in place to achieve your goals, they are pure fantasy."

Every situation contains a *SURPRISE* component. It's been found that moments of testing always yield something far greater. Just keep going, keep rising, and keep believing, no matter how things appear. The VISION within you will carry you through. I've received more energy, which has always inspired me to CREATE, DREAM, and MANIFEST everything my heart truly desires...*THAT WAS MY TURNING POINT...*

My biggest turning point and learning curve came when I entered the automobile industry. A business industry is dominated by large and powerful corporations, but Nature sometimes shows us how a much smaller, but intelligent entity can drive out power. To enter the automobile market, I chose **luxury retail**, which outperforms the non-luxury segment significantly. The eagle had a profound influence on me. I observed that the crow is the only bird brave enough to tease it. Instead of fighting the crow, the eagle spreads his wings and soars higher until the crow is unable to breathe at such altitudes and crashes to the ground. My most important takeaway was that not all battles, arguments, or criticisms needed to be fought or responded to. Simply alter your trajectory, as I did, and devise a survival strategy in a market dominated by large and powerful competitors.

What is entrepreneurship?

Here's how **Harvard Business School** defines entrepreneurship - "It's a RELENTLESS pursuit of OPPORTUNITIES without regard to RESOURCES currently controlled."

Their unwavering pursuits are motivated by a strong desire to succeed. They are passionate, business-savvy, and confident planners with whatever resources they have, always on the lookout for opportunities with a never-say-die attitude. While there is no rocket science formula for a good entrepreneur, they are a bundle of managerial skills, a leader who encourages teamwork through sound communication and analytical skills, a strong focus on their vision, an eagerness to learn, and a high level of adaptability.

Who is an aspiring entrepreneur?

People ask me, what is the purpose of Business?

And I respond:

In a nutshell, the real purpose of a business is NOT to create profits. Because a business cannot exist outside of society and must satisfy a specific need in order to stay in business, it has to create or add additional value to the community or individuals. That's why the real purpose of a business is to create customers. Is it to create profits? Yes, one of the objective of any business is to earn a profit. Just as a plant cannot survive without water, similarly a business cannot sustain without profit. Profit is necessary for growing and expanding business activities.

Be your own boss? Supporting an advocacy? Provide a community a livelihood?

All these are great vision and mission statements.

One day my heart is going to stop, and that will be the end of my body-- but not the end of my Business

While end-of-life may seem scary, it's a natural part of the business life cycle. With innovation comes new technology. As new technologies emerge, old ones become less useful and less attractive to customers. This is normal! However, end-of-life can have serious implications for businesses. This means that companies must either upgrade their technology or accept the risks of not doing so. - and until you figure that out, business isn't going to make sense.

Business has its own series of problems: Either you are in one now, or you're just coming out of one, or you're getting ready to go into another one. The reason for this is that this experience makes you tough in your character and pulls you out of your comfort;

We can be reasonably happy, but that's not the goal of my entrepreneurship the goal is to grow in character, Business goals can take many different forms and be aspirational or motivational, such as driving an organization toward a certain objective like improved customer service. And to achieve these goals, no matter how good things are in your life, there is always something bad that needs to be worked on.

And no matter how bad things are in your life, there is always something good you can be proud for.

Be focus on your purpose, and not on your problems:

If you focus on your problems, you're going into self-centeredness, which is your problem, your issues, your pain. But one of the easiest ways to get rid of pain is to get your focus off yourself and onto the Goal and vision and mission of your entrepreneurial journey

We need to ask ourselves: Am I going to live for Wealth generation? Popularity?

Or Am I going to be driven by pressures? Guilt? Bitterness? Materialism?

- Happy moments, PRAISE GOD.
- Difficult moments, SEEK GOD.
- Quiet moments, WORSHIP GOD.
- Painful moments, TRUST GOD.
- Every moment, THANK GOD.

An entrepreneur DOES NOT SIT AND TALK ABOUT 'IDEAS. He/she is always on the move and starting something new. He/she is constantly looking for ways to put his/her ideas into action. You have no idea how ideas evolve and become great over time.

(Source: Internet)

(Source: Internet)

In addition, an entrepreneur is always on the lookout to acquire knowledge and information, and he/she is a quick learner. Knowledge is like a horizon to him/her, and the more you share and apply it, the more you get.

Personally, I think ...

Knowledge is superior to wealth: *Knowledge guards you, whereas you guard wealth. Wealth decreases with expenditure, whereas knowledge multiplies with dissemination. Thanks to knowledge, you command people's respect. Knowledge rules over wealth. Those who treasure wealth perish while they are still alive,* *whereas scholars live forever! Their memories are enshrined in their hearts.*

Spend your time learning and expanding your knowledge. Understanding comes with knowledge, and life is put into perspective. It's going to be extremely difficult as the road is never easy, but bumpy rides make you experienced. You can either quit it early or choose to keep going, keep rising, and keep believing no matter what... Not everyone is meant to run a business or launch a start-up.

Yes, doing business in India is difficult. When it comes to sales, your ego and all of your high-degree credential tags will crumble - especially in business-to-business (B2B) where you speak directly with your customers. In business-to-customer (B2C), you don't see your customers, but the analytics can be discouraging. The customer is the most important person in any business. He is the king, and if he is happy, you are happy. Take in a lot of feedback from him/her to improve your product or service. You'll be amazed to find them taking out time to help you. The Golden Rule demands that every customer and situation be treated with kindness and thoughtfulness. Such consideration of others can lead to companies performing better than expected.

NICEF, UNESCO and WHO list the ten core life skill strategies and techniques which are equally core to Business success as: problem solving, critical thinking, effective communication skills, decision-making, creative thinking, interpersonal relationship skills, self- awareness building skills, empathy, and coping with stress and emotions.

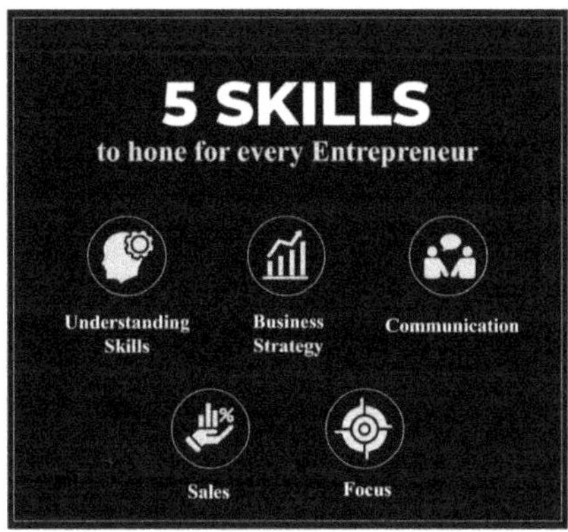

The most important skill is SALES

People believe that their coding/tech skills, as well as their 'tags,' are sufficient to run a start-up, however, this is not the case. They save you from hassles, but are clearly not necessary. You need to learn sales, negotiation, pitching, etc. You learn this by actually doing it.

A sales team is a team of people, who perform their duties to the best of their abilities. It has nothing to do with the industry, but it has lots to do with the skillset of the person doing the job.

During my stint within the automobile industry, I have observed that a person who can sell 10 units of budget cars might not be able to perform the same way as compared to a person selling luxury cars and vice versa. It is their passion for selling combined with their sales skills that allow them to do their job effectively.

The attitude and ability to sell are at the heart of the process. The best example would be automobiles, where you sell dreams and emotions to aspiring buyers by connecting and providing them with solutions in the form of their dream purchases.

In my opinion, the best sales team is one that believes in after-sales service and brims with optimism, regardless of industry. When you have a client who has been pitched, converted, and satisfied and who gives you additional references, you have achieved the best sales with the best team and the best work.

The sales team is the mirror of every company/organization/industry, it is also important in bridging the gap between customers and the company, brand, and product or service. Every industry, in my opinion, values having a high-quality sales team.

Employee satisfaction

Employees are an organization's true assets. They are the ones who contribute effectively toward the successful functioning of an organization. They strive hard to deliver their level best and achieve the assigned targets within a stipulated time. Employee satisfaction is an essential aspect of any business or organization. When employees are happy and satisfied with the management and work culture, they put their best effort to make the company successful.

Hey Mr. Budding Entrepreneur, tell your employees I'm always with you. ASSURE THEM: "If you're alone, I'll be your shadow. If you want to cry, I'll be your shoulder. If you want a hug, I'll be your pillow. If you need to be happy, I'll be your smile... But if you need a friend, I'll just be myself, NOT YOUR CEO OR BOSS, BUT YOUR COLLEAGUE, GUIDE, AND MENTOR."

Humsafar bhi hain, humraaz bhi,
Humshakal bhi hain, humzuban bhi,
Kyon farq kartey hain sab unmein aur hum mein,
Woh to humnafas bhi hain humwatan bhi!

Translation:
We are co-travellers (here it refers to colleagues) and share the same secrets,
We have the same look and speak the same tongue,
Then why do we differentiate between them and us (referring to employer and employee here)
We are of the same spirit and belong to the same Nation (referring to organisation)!

Good things are easy to buy, but good people are difficult to find. Life ends when you stop dreaming, hope ends when you stop believing, and love ends when you stop caring and sharing. Your employee requires a caring and sharing employer. The employer-employee relationship is the key to success in any business venture.

If you judge people, nobody is yours.
If you understand people, everyone is yours.
Develop the habit of understanding,
And you will experience peace and love in all relations.

Employee involvement is the key to a successful venture. A sense of ownership makes employees feel a part of an organization. They become more responsible about their work and push themselves to find better results. This enhances their role-play and possibilities of innovative thinking and ideas to tackle problems in the workplace. It's important for a business owner to recognize a job well done by an employee and facilitate a respectful relationship.

Likewise, **Networking** is essential for increasing the visibility of your organisation, meeting new people, and developing social skills.While mentoring, I always advise CEOs to get out there and talk to people in order to get to know their employees. This exercise will not only help you become a better entrepreneur, but it will also help you improve your social skills and make you a better person. According to studies conducted all over the world, being connected to business associates, friends, families, and the community makes us happier; this, in turn, leads to longer, healthier, and more fruitful lives. While loneliness is a killer, it will also kill your business; instead, let us focus on making our relationships, lives, and businesses happier and longer-lasting.

Community is important. We should know others in our business as well as local areas and help them when possible, especially in times of pandemic. If a person does not have enough and has been cut off from the community to the point where no one knows when they are in need, they are truly at a loss. Connect with others in any way you can. Remember that even a smile is a form of charity.

The best way to celebrate your success is to celebrate the way the poor and needy celebrate. Empathy and compassion are the need of the day. Meet other entrepreneurs and investors; this will provide you with ideas and ensure that you receive adequate visibility and support. It also serves as a learning experience for you by allowing you to share your thoughts and vision.

Brand building exercise

Building a brand requires clear brand core values, unequivocal positioning, and a long-term strategy. When a brand becomes tangible over a long period of time, it is considered strong. To build a brand through good market research, you must first determine your brand personality and your product's strong positioning. It is critical to establish your brand identity through architecture and trademarks. Most importantly, ensure that you deliver on the brand promise.

So, how do you build a brand? First and foremost, define your brand mission, then determine your target audience and profile your audience through proper research and competition. Create a value proposition and your own brand guidelines.

Finally, and most importantly, grow a tough skin. People would either think you're an idiot (when you first start) or be envious of you (when you start showing signs of success). People will say, write, and read nonsense about you, but you must believe in yourself.

Remember the words of famous artist James de la Vega *"Whoever wishes to win in this game must have patience and money, since the values are so little constant and the rumours so little founded on truth."*

Believe and appreciate your own expertise and experience as those are the results of struggles, experiments, and even tears.

Also, remember what Sallust, a Roman historian and one of the great Latin literary stylists,stated in 86 BC – 34 BC, *"They envy the distinction I have won; let them, therefore, envy my toils, my honesty, and the methods by which I gained it.*

III

BUSINESS ENTREPRENEURS IN THE MAKING 2.0

A Right Approach towards Success and Failure

Sometimes it's not the pain that makes us suffer. It is our own negative thoughts that make things seem even worse. Remember that ease is bound to come after every hardship. Fix your attitude. Trust in God, clear your mind and stay positive.

An Honest Intention:
- Helps establish sincerity.
- Enables proper purpose for action.
- Gives inner strength.
- Moves one to a goal.
- Assists in formalizing action.
- Facilitates blessings

Our lives improve only when we take chances, and the first and most difficult risk we can take is to be honest with ourselves.

We are Programmed for successes but not trained for handling failures. And failures lead to Depression, Anxiety which can happen to any of us. It's a sad reality. However, the last few years coupled with the recent pandemic have been instrumental in accelerating the urgency for mental health awareness. That being healthy and having a structured life allowed you to make the best use of the opportunities that came your way. Working probably for 20 hours a day, should not stop you from being active in business ventures even then, which means, you work relentlessly and, never tired, but wanted to do something else also... you might fail a lot but also success will follow as you have the mental and physical bandwidth to do it all. Most importantly, (fitness) will help you to maintain discipline in everything else what you have done, what fitness actually means - it is the ability to carry out all the responsibilities through the day without any mental or physical strain and living without any major ailments, a healthy heart, no gut issues and not even minor ailments like chronic backache and acidity. That the definition of fitness has moved beyond getting six-pack abs, flat stomachs or getting one's weight in control. "It's about being in a great space which is also very mental. Being fit and healthy will have the most positive impact on your life, professionally, is just a bonus.... Following a pandemic that changed the world as we knew it -- we owe this to our family and ourselves, Mental Health has largely remained in the fringes in India, due to its deep-rooted stigma, taboo, and myths. This has resulted in limited access to mental health services and shortage of such specialists, hence as an entrepreneur its essential to reach out to each other and help each other through whatever means possible.

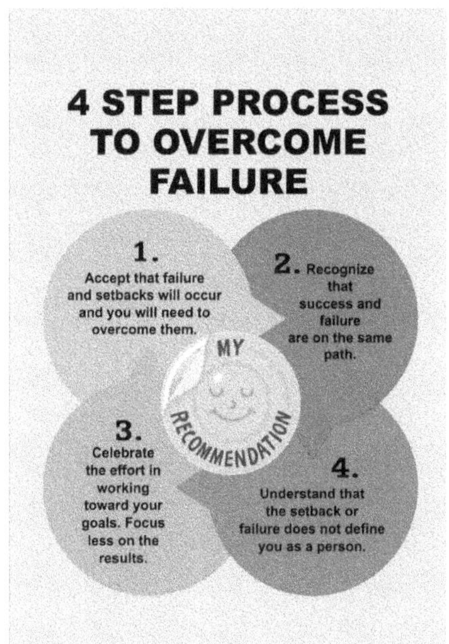

"Depression, anxiety and panic attacks are not signs of weakness. They are sign of illness." Mental health is not a stigma: But to not have your suffering recognized and diagnosed is an almost unbearable form of violence."

Depression can be dangerous. Bit by bit, day by day it can slowly grow before it overwhelms & controls you. Be positive in every outlook of your life. If you feel life isn't as planned, be assured that you are exactly where God wants you to be. And He is the best of planners.

Life is simple indeed
But We make it complex by running after what NEVER gives us joy....
Love life
Take note of small things...!!!
Keep Smiling

Zindagi pal-pal dhalti hai ......
Jaise ret mutthi se fisalti hai ....
Shikwe kitne bhi ho har pal fir bhi haste rehna ...

Kyonki yeh zindagi jaisi bhi hai ..
Bas ek hi bar Milti hai

Translation: Life goes on moment by moment......
Like the slipping of the mud from fist
No matter how many complaints you have, keep smiling every moment...
Because life is like that...
You only get it once

Unfortunately, the clock is ticking, the hours are going by.
The past increases, the future recedes.
Possibilities decreasing, regrets mounting.
The timeless in you is aware of life's timelessness.
And knows that yesterday is but today's memory and tomorrow is today's dream.
Now let's come to the actual question, what are the habits of highly successful Business man?

As a starting point, it's helpful to know that success is typically defined as reaching a goal or accomplishing something you've set out to achieve. It provides a source of motivation for people to change their lives and values. Passion, Vision, Preparation, Courage, Perseverance and Integrity, set you on to your individual paths to success. By learning ad taking control of these four habits you can become a successful person,

- To Have Great Self Concept.
- To be Consistent.
- Step Out of your Comfort Zone.

To be Positive Thinkers.

First of all, there are many people who will say you about success habits but today I am saying you even if you have achieved everything there is always a chance to lose everything, nobody knows when the next pandemic, or Economic Crisis will hit the world. The best success habit according to me is getting trained for handling failures...

I also request every Entrepreneur, to not only program your next generation to be successful but teach them how to handle failures and also teach them proper lessons about life. Learning high-level science and maths will help them to clear competitive exams but A knowledge about Life will help them to face every problem. Teach them about how money works instead of teaching them to work for money. Help them in finding their passion because these degrees will not help them in the next economics or pandemic crisis and we don't know when the next crisis hit the world.

1) Short-term pleasures can lead to long-term traps.
2) If things are coming easy and you are getting comfortable, you are getting trapped into dependency.

3) When you are not using your skills, you will lose more than your skills. You lose your CHOICES and FREEDOM.

4) Freedom does not come easy but can be lost very quickly.

NOTHING comes easily in life and if it comes easily, maybe it is not worth it.

There are no free lunches

Remember the Mouse in a jar full of Grains. Very Happy to see so much of food easily available. No need to run around, but can't see this short-term happiness as Long-term trap. After few days enjoying the sit home meal, he reaches the bottom of the jar, and now he is trapped. Now he becomes dependent on someone to fill the jar with grains, and that too of not his choice, so don't be complacent and over dependent.

Be Cautious and Avoid

Fear
Envy
Anger
Hatred

So, what is Fear; Envy; Anger; Hatred

A Turkish Poet Jalaluddin Rumi has beautiful answers for this

- **Fear** is: Non-Acceptance of Uncertainty…but if we accept that Uncertainty it becomes Adventure
- **Envy** is: Non-Acceptance of Good in others. but if we accept that Good its Inspiration
- **Anger** is: Non-Acceptance of Things which are beyond our control, but if we accept its Tolerance
- **Hatred** is: Non-acceptance of Person as he is, but if we accept it unconditionally its Love

I am really inclined to share this one of the most beautiful and amazing advice by the great scholar Imam Ibn al-Qayyim (rahimahullah)

A friend will not share your struggles, and a loved one cannot physically take away your pain, and a close one will not stay up the night on your behalf.

So, look after yourself, protect yourself, nurture yourself and don't give life's events more than what they are really worth. Know for certain that when you break no one will heal you except you, and when you are defeated no one will give you victory except your determination.

Your ability to stand up again and carry on is your responsibility. Do not look for your self-worth in the eyes of people; look for your worth from within your conscience.

If your conscience is at peace then you will ascend high and if you truly know yourself then what is said about you won't harm you.

Live your life with this principle. "Be good even if you don't receive good, not because of others' sake but because God loves those who do good"

The highest courage is to dare to be yourself in the face of adversity. Choosing right over wrong, ethics over convenience and truth over popularity. These are the choices that measure your life. Travel the path of integrity without looking back, for there is never a wrong time to do the right thing.

This is what I say as LION Mode

1. You don't need to be the fastest.
2. You don't need to be the wisest.
3. You don't need to be the smartest.
4. You don't need to be the most brilliant.
5. All you need is *courage*
6. All you need is the *will to try*.
7. All you need is the *faith* to believe it *is possible*.
8. All you need is to believe in yourself, that *you can* do it.!!

These are the attributes of Lion Mode. We have come across this example multiple times but never thought of it...Let's now ponder over it....

In the jungle:
1. The Elephant is the biggest
2. The Giraffe is the tallest
3. The Fox is the wisest
4. The Cheetah is the fastest

Yet, the Lion is the KING of the jungle even without ANY of these qualities. Why?

Because:

1. The Lion is courageous, is bold, walks with confidence, dares anything and is never afraid.
2. The Lion believes it is unstoppable.
3. The Lion is a risk taker.
4. The Lion believes any animal is food for him.
5. The Lion believes any opportunity is worth giving a try and never lets it slip from its hands.

Stay in Lion Mode! That's the mode for winners!

Lion Mode should guide you throughout your Entrepreneurial life.........

Once you are in Lion's Mode and adopted the attributes of the King of Jungle, now let's take off and fly in the journey of Entrepreneurial skies by understanding the path of uninterrupted horizon from my King of Skies an Eagle. Again, we have come across this classic example but never thought of how nature gives us lessons of lifetime

Have you seen Eagles, they fly Alone and at High Altitudes?

They don't fly with sparrows, ravens, and other small birds.

-Stay away from narrow-minded people, those that bring you down. Eagle flies with Eagles.

Keep good company.

Eagles have an Accurate Vision. They have the ability to focus on something as far as 5km away. No matter the obstacles, the eagle will not move his focus from the prey until he grabs it.

-Have a vision and remain focused no matter what the obstacles and you will succeed.

Eagles do not Eat Dead things. They Feed only on Fresh Prey.

-Do not rely on your past success, keep looking for new frontiers to conquer. Leave your past where it belongs, in the past.

Eagles Love the Storm.

When clouds gather, the eagle gets excited, the eagle uses the storms wind to lift itself higher. Once it finds the wind of the storm, the eagle uses the raging storm to lift itself above the clouds. This gives the eagle an opportunity to glide and rest its wings. In the meantime, all the other birds hide in the branches and leaves of the tree.

-Face your challenges head on knowing that these will make you emerge stronger and better than you were. We can use the storms of life to rise to greater heights. Achievers are not afraid to rise to greater heights. Achievers are not afraid of challenges, rather they relish them and use them profitably.

When a Female Eagle Meets a Male Eagle* and they want to mate, she flies down to earth, picks a twig and flies back into the air with the male eagle in hot pursuit. Once she has reached a height high enough for her, she drops the twig and let it fall to the ground while she watches. The male eagle chases after the twig and catches it before it reached the ground, then bring it back to the female eagle. The female eagle grabs the twig and flies to a much higher altitude and drops the twig again for the male eagle to chase. This goes on for hours with the height increasing each time until the female eagle is assured that the male eagle has mastered the art of picking the twig which shows commitment. Then and only then will she allow him to mate with her.

-Whether in private life or business, one should test the commitment of the people intended
for partnership.

Eagles Prepare for Training;

They remove the feathers and soft grass in the nest so that the young ones get uncomfortable in preparation for flying and eventually flies when it becomes unbearable to stay in the nest.

-Leave your Comfort Zone, there is No Growth there.

When the Eagle Grows Old,

His feathers become weak and cannot take him as fast and as high as it should. This makes him weak and could make him die. So, he retires to a place far away in the mountains. While there, he plucks out the weak feathers on his body and breaks its beaks and claws against the rocks until he is completely bare; a very bloody and painful process. Then he stays in this hiding place until he has grown new feathers, new beaks and claws and then he comes out flying higher than before.

-We occasionally need to shed off old habit no matter how difficult, things that burden us or
add no value to our lives should be let go of.

*YES, NEVER GIVE UP, *
BE AN EAGLE, NEVER EVER GIVE UP !!!

Body Language in a Successful Entrepreneurship:

Business relationships are built on communication. ...

Body language in business sets the foundation for people to communicate with others on a deeper level. From your facial expressions to your body movements, the things that you don't say can often convey some of the largest volumes of information.

Body language is the use of physical behavior, expressions, and mannerisms to communicate non-verbally, often done instinctively rather than consciously. ... All of your non-verbal behaviors—the gestures you make, your posture, your tone of voice, how much eye contact you make—send strong messages.

Types of Body Movement

All people express their body language in one of four ways: a light and bouncy movement, a soft and fluid movement, a dynamic and determined movement, or a precise and bold movement.

Importance of Body language

The importance of body language is that it assists us in understanding and decoding what the person is saying. Body language also helps interpret other peoples' moods and emotions. Apart from this, it enhances our conscious understanding of people's reactions to what we say and how we say it.

Example of body language communication

Your arms and legs are perhaps one of the first types of non-verbal communication that people notice when they see you. You can use them for positive body language or negative body language. Sitting or standing with your arms crossed across your chest is nearly always seen as defensive body language.

Positive Body Language

Positive body language can be defined as these nonverbal movements and gestures that are communicating interest, enthusiasm, and positive reactions to what someone else is saying. ... To many, body language is considered the most important aspect of communication as it sends signals to how we are truly feeling.

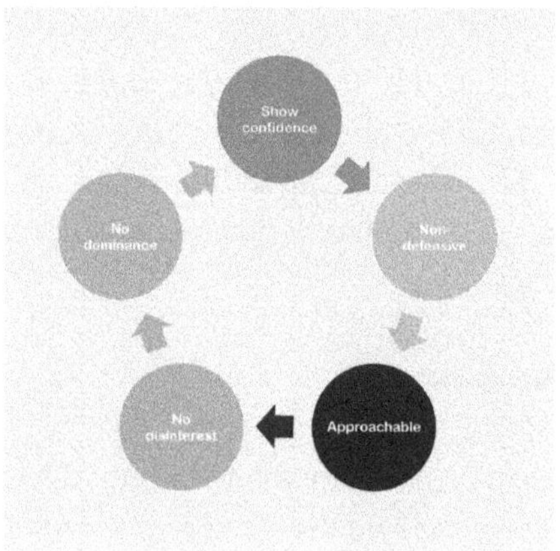

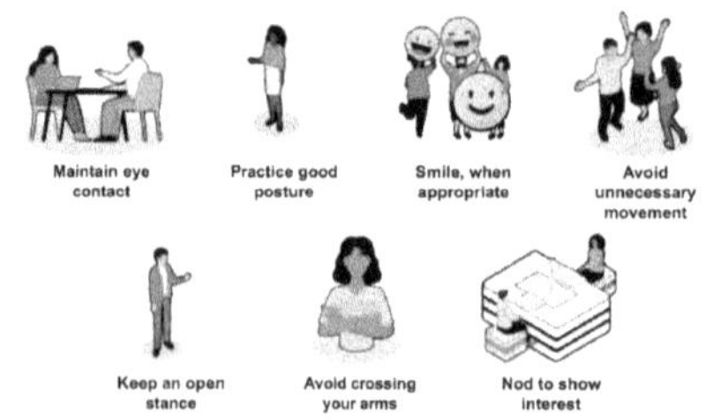

Examples of positive body language

Maintain good eye contact. Maintaining good eye contact shows you're engaged and actively listening to what someone is telling you. ...

- Head nod. ...
- Firm handshake. ...
- Open palms. ...
- Upright and open posture. ...
- Leaning in while speaking (and listening) ...
- Minimal facial expressions. ...

Rapid blinking.

Confident Body language

A confident person literally has two feet firmly planted on the ground," Glass says. "You're more balanced physically, and it shows more confidence than if your legs are crossed or together." Also keep in mind the difference between an open and closed stance when talking to some one

Negative Body language

Negative body language is either a conscious or unconscious expression of sadness, anger, nervousness, impatience, boredom, or lack of confidence. ... Types of negative body language include: Avoidance of eye contact.

Where the entrepreneur goes wrong......THE FAULTY LINES IN AN ENTREPRENEURIAL JOURNEY

From my experience with startups and young entrepreneurs, I'm sharing here the biggest mistakes they make hoping that this information will help the young entrepreneurs establish a successful business.

Source: (Internet)

Keeping their idea, a secret

Many young entrepreneurs prefer not to disclose their business idea with anyone so as to prevent the risk of getting their idea stolen. This is the biggest mistake they make.

If you do not share your idea with anyone, you would never come to know if the idea is suitable as per the market needs, does the business idea needs any improvements, is there any company existing with the same idea, etc. Thus, you miss the opportunity to start with a better idea or prevent becoming a replica of some other brand.

It's true you should share your business idea, but should also consider with whom you are sharing and to which extent. I prefer sharing the basic idea only; not the modules. And in case you are sharing the whole idea, make sure you are done with proper documentation so that you can prove your copyright on that idea.

No Clear Vision

Many people just get moved by the feeling of becoming their own boss; they have no idea of what to do and how. They lack vision, do not come up with a required business plan and so, suffer later.

Lack of Focus

In the hurry to become successful, many young entrepreneurs start with so many business plans or even get into different businesses. This is not the right way. Successful entrepreneur is the one who has established a successful startup, and not the one who has many businesses. Also, success is not something you can get overnight; it needs patience and continuous efforts.

Doing everything all alone

Young entrepreneurs feel they do not need anyone's help; everything can be done by themselves. This mistake can make your startup fail. Though you might be capable of doing everything, but it is always better to have a team who doubles the quality work and halves the time taken. With the time saved from the tasks associated with building business, you can go out, make connections, share your views, get their valuable advices and ultimately promote your brand.

Craving for Perfection…. Mr. Perfectionist

Young entrepreneurs often wish to make their product perfect and then launch or wait for the right time, hardly they know that there's nothing like perfection; all that matters are the speed and adaptability. If you go with the latest trends and hit the market much before your competitors, you are likely to earn more profit than others.

Unwilling to admit their mistake…. Mr. Always Right

Many young entrepreneurs feel that they are perfect and turn deaf ears to others advices and suggestions. This is one of the dreadful mistakes made by entrepreneurs. It is okay to make mistakes, but one should admit his/her mistake and take the lesson from it so as to undo the future danger.

CASE STUDY:

Over a last couple of years, I had opportunity to mentor some Startups in the field of Sales and Marketing. After minutely studying and understanding the concept of a startup in high end Retail I have few points for you to think and elaborate among your team for basically sustaining the growth of a company

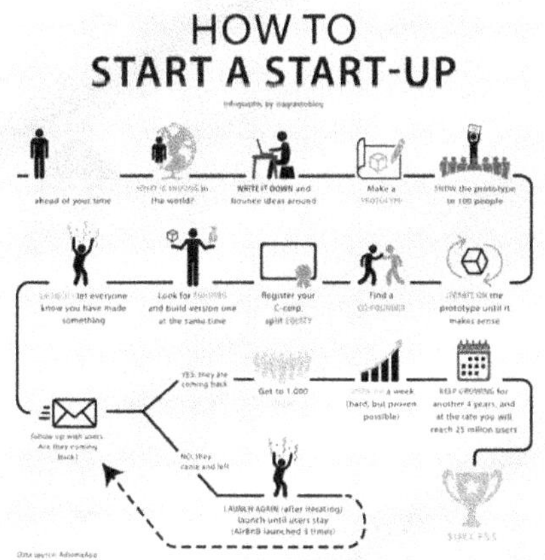

Source : (Internet)

1. **Marketing:**

After running a business for couple of years and looking to the product profile, what you need is more exposure and focus on your Marketing strategies, because according to my understanding, just a business and its operational skills are not enough to gain ground in a successful entrepreneurship, but it's a collective process of Operations, Business, Finance and Marketing. And above all how these four elements and its ideas are implemented. We have plethora of ideas, specially among the startups, but they stumble on implementation.

The Key to Marketing is its strategy and implementation Plan. **For Detail Refer Appendix Section {D}**

1. **Revenue:**

What I have realized in my entire business life, that understanding the product and customer is one thing, but to set up a sustainable business is entirely different. For you and your team one thing I can vouch that you may be very well in control of the products, which I would say could be your core competency, and also suppose you have very well identified customer base, but to sustain, is a million-dollar question. This is where sales and marketing and brand building comes in to place for a long and everlasting sustainability. Generally, the startup entrepreneurs don't understand that it is not a linear game. What you do to get your angel investor, will not at all work for the next big-ticket investor. We tend to focus on top line (revenue) without understanding the power of the bottom line (net profits), this is where you need to know the intricacies of running a successful business, and this is what attracts the long-term investor.

3. **Customer Centric approach:**

Customer is the most important visitor on our premises. He is not dependent on us. We are dependent on him. He is not an interruption on our work. He is the purpose of it. He is not an outsider on our business. He is part of it. We are not doing him a favour by serving him. He is doing us a favor by giving us an opportunity to do so. ~ Mahatma Gandhi

4. **Financial Stability:**

Become financially responsible, it takes ages to earn wealth, but only seconds to squander it. Overcome the "poverty mind-set" that you will never have enough money when you have the power to change that reality. Seek out a financial planner who can help you realise the value of money and bring your goals on track. Invest in learning as much as you can about financial planning and personal finance so that your wealth does not slip out of your hands like sand, all because of some poor money choices and adverse life events. Take your first step, today. As Robert Kiyosaki puts it, "It's not how much money you make, but how much money you keep, how hard it works for you, and how many generations you keep it for." Making money is much easier than preserving and saving it for the long term. And let's face it, we all face rough patches in our lives, where financial stress can be overwhelming, as was the case with Cairns.

Getting your money to work for you even in times like these can be tough, but you can get an edge by setting aside an emergency fund, the purpose of which will be to help you tide over tough times without having to dip into your investments. Ideally, an emergency fund should cover all compulsory expenses for at least 6-12 months with a comfortable margin for any unanticipated expenditure.

IV

BUSINESS DEALINGS IN AN ETHICAL WAY

"**Morality does not rely on religion**" "A man's ethical behaviour should be based effectually on sympathy, education, and social ties and needs; no religious basis is necessary.

Theethical form of business and Trade includes Freedom, Justice, mannerism, and consideration of others need. Whereas according to my understanding and belief the disapproved business conducts are interest based finance, Fraud, dishonesty, and dealing in prohibited commodities.

According to my understanding definition of business ethics is the set of moral rules that govern how business operate, how business decisions are made and how people are treated...these moral rules applied by organisation to determine how best to treat its employees, stakeholders and customers. Ethics is what guides us to tell the truth, keep our promises, or help someone in need. There is a framework of ethics underlying our lives on a daily basis, helping us make decisions that create positive impacts and steering us away from unjust outcomes. Without a strong set of ethics, a business can run afoul of the law, encounter financial pitfalls and moral dilemmas.

Business ethics inform a company's values and goals, as well as how it runs its day-to-day operations. An ethical company runs on principles such as honesty, integrity, fairness, trustworthiness, accountability, and respect for others. Engage, communicate and train your staff. Engage staff and other stakeholders such as suppliers, investors, regulators and consumer communities, through effective and informative communication. Good, regular and consistent communication and training will help to embed an ethical culture.

LAYOFFS AND TOXIC WORK CULTURE ARE BUZZWORDS TODAY. Other various Types of Ethical Issues in Business are:

- Discrimination. One of the biggest ethical issues affecting the business world in 2020 is discrimination.
- Harassment.
- Unethical Accounting. ...
- Health and Safety.
- Abuse of Leadership Authority.
- Nepotism and Favouritism.
- Privacy.
- Corporate Espionage

If your company is going through a tough time, the best recourse is to care for your employees. They may not remember what actions you took, but they will remember how they were treated. (Ashira Gobrin. Forbes). The more true and supportive you be emotionally as well as financially towards your team the more you win them and thus you earn them. The justice, honesty, fairness, generosity and trust are among the ethical behaviours suggested by the Islam. With these behaviour, employees could create a conducive environment in the workplace and motivate the development of better performance. Religious ethics form a major part of broader understandings of ethical issues. Many religions and denominations apply both an ethical screen to investment and also advocate specific ethical approaches to business.

Business dealings Islamic way

Islam permits only for legitimate business as Quran tells us, "**O you who believe: Eat not up your property among yourselves unjustly except it may be trade among you by mutual consent**" (part no 5, surah no 4 verse no 29.)

Islam places great emphasis on regulation and business ethics in human life. Ethics as a rule good or bad, right or wrong, moral teachings about behaviour and actions, especially in the economy comes out to the Muslim faith. Whatever is done will be linked to the objective world and hereafter.

Islam greatly encourages business, as it directly contributes to improving the standard of living and providing worldly comforts to mankind. Sources of livelihood are in business, for their business activities as long as they obey the commands of God, and the smallest good deed will be recognised and rewarded. Successful Muslim entrepreneurs are driven by a strong desire to help and serve people through their products and services. Your business will succeed to the extent that you provide value to the marketplace. The more value you provide, the more money you will make. It's that simple.

Prophet Muhammad was known as Al-Amin, or "The Trustworthy."

He earned this name based on his reputation as a successful merchant.

Prophet Muhammad said: "Speak the truth, keep your promises, fulfil your trusts."

It was Prophet Muhammad (may peace be upon him) who, on the one hand, urged his followers to adopt trade as their profession, and, on the other band, exhorted them to observe truthfulness and honesty in their business transactions.

Empowering words. Truthfulness is the foundation of all human virtues.

The Prophet, peace and blessings be upon him, said, "Both parties in a business transaction have the right to annul it, as long as they have not separated. If they are truthful and clear with one another, there is blessing in their transaction. If they lie and conceal something, the blessing of their transaction will be eliminated."

Source: S.ah.ih. al-Bukhārī 1973, S.ah.ih. Muslim 1532

The Prophet (blessings and peace of Allah be upon him) worked in business before his mission began, with his paternal uncle Abu Taalib, and he also worked for Khadijah, and he travelled for that purpose to greater Syria. He also did business in the markets; Majannah and 'Ukaaz were markets during the pre-prophet hood days to which merchants would come to buy and sell.

The Prophet (blessings and peace of Allah be upon him) used to engage directly in transactions himself, he also used to appoint one of his companions to do that for him,

Once Prophet (blessings and peace of Allah be upon him) gave one of his companion one dinar to buy a sacrificial animal or a sheep for him. Companion bought two sheep and sold one for one dinar, and he came back with a sheep and a dinar. The Prophet (blessings and peace of Allah be upon him)) prayed for blessing for him in his business dealings, and (after that) if he had bought dust he would have made a profit.

- "When a sale is held, say, "There's no cheating." (Book: Al-Bukhari).
- "Be careful of excessive oaths in a sale. Though it finds markets, it reduces abundance." (Book: Muslim).
- "The sale is complete when the two parties involved depart with mutual consent." (Book: Al-Bukhari).
- "When people cheat in weight and measures, their provision is cut off from them" (Book: Al-Muwatta).
- "You (Business people) have been entrusted with affairs over which some nations before you were destroyed" (Book: Al-Tirmidhi).
- "Whoever monopolizes is a sinner" (Book: Abu Dawud).

Furthermore, the Prophet says that in the case of free enterprise, the price of the commodities shouldn't be fixed, say there is a situational crisis or utmost necessity, Prophet prohibited hoarding merchandise so as to increase the prices in the market. He also forbade the transaction of prohibited items in Islam, such as alcohol, drugs and intoxicants.

Islam imposes limits on possession, ownership and consumption. Its law of inheritance diffuses accrued personal holdings. Both the Quran and the Hadith denounce display of one's resourcefulness through extravagant lifestyle.

Performing a religious obligation is up to you and it is something between you and your God. However, good ethics is something between you and other people. In other words, if we do not put our ethics into action and practice, corruption will become rampant.

We should not judge a person based on how he performs religious obligations for he might be a hypocrite.

The Prophet Muhammad (peace be upon him) said: "Verily, the bankrupt of my nation is those who come on the Day of Judgement with lots of prayers, fasting and charity, but also have insulted, slander, consuming wealth, shedding and beating others."

Ethical is all about how we Treat Others

Have you ever observed the difference between some of the Rich and advanced countries?

What I feel is their attitude of the people, moulded for years by education and moral culture.

Take the example of Japan, totally finished after world war II, but bounced back to become among the top 3 economies of the world. It's like a floating factory, importing raw material from across the world and exporting its manufactured good worldwide.

Switzerland, a snow-capped country, hardly for 4 months in a year can cultivate its land, and rear its animal, but produces among the best dairy products. Surprisingly does not grow Cocoa, but makes world best chocolates. Developed its fool-proof security systems, and created its niche in worlds best private Banks.

When we analyze the conduct of the people from the rich and developed countries, it is observed that a majority abide by the following principles of Business and life:

1. Ethics, as basic principles.
2. Integrity.
3. Responsibility.
4. The respect for Laws and Regulations.
5. The respect from majority of citizens by right.
6. The love for work.
7. The effort to save and invest.
8. The will to be productive.
9. Punctuality.

Let's consciously ask this to ourselves.... Do we follow these basic principles in our daily life?

No, we don't....... because we lack attitude. We lack the will to follow and learn these principles of developed societies.

WE ARE IN THIS STATE BECAUSE
WE WANT TO TAKE ADVANTAGE OVER
EVRYTHING AND EVERYONE.

WE ARE IN THIS STATE BECAUSE
WE SEE SOMETHING DONE WRONG
AND SAY - "LET IT BE" Chalta hai attitude
WE SHOULD HAVE A SPIRITED MEMORY AND ATTITUDE...
ONLY THEN WILL WE BE ABLE TO CHANGE OUR PRESENT STATE.

Today India, which gave to the world the earliest and the most enlightened concept of Trade and Business, has totally gone into oblivion from the international business scene

Yet today, we are not even considered a community of Business Repute. We are way behind in Ease of Doing Business Why? What has reversed the course of our journey? We have badly faltered in our trade ethical practices.

What are they?
Certain key and basic practices are:

I. To accept sold goods back without a blink of an eye
II. Clearly mark any fault, blemish or distortion in the product.

III. Not to make any false claims or praise too much about one's product
IV. Transparency and standardization of the product

What an enigma?

These present day Western Business have just replicated these ethical practices and the result is in front of us. Any of us can just ponder into these businesses either through a Supermarket, online business companies like Amazon etc. or any other service industry, we are more comfortable buying their product than any other.

Therefore, to overcome this enigma we need to show courage, honesty and integrity.

If you plant honesty, you will reap trust!
If you plant goodness, you will reap friends!
If you plant humility, you will reap greatness!
If you plant perseverance, you will reap contentment!
If you plant consideration, you will reap perspective!
If you plant hard work, you will reap success!

If you plant forgiveness, you will reap reconciliation!
Be careful in what you plant now, for it will determine what you reap later!

Financial Conduct

Most of us consider that a huge amount of money, as well as a highly equipped best team of experts or professionals, is necessary to start a business. But according to historiographer and modern scholars to start any business the only thing required is passion and skills.

According to many scholars, the significance and the depth of the word Tajir are more than the word Entrepreneur so it is better to use the word Tajir because the word is not limited in its value system. The first rule of business is to practice this essential principle: The belief that God will give you the best if you put in the work.

Success and achievements in business come to those who have a clear vision of their dreams, those make every effort in an Ethical way towards it and do what it takes to next level or heights of success.

So, another key word we need to address is long term financial planning and management, how important long-term perspective can be.

Financial discipline is the basic requirement, best of entrepreneurs have failed due to financial mismanagement, both on individual basis as well as for Business enterprise, we need to capitalize all our resources onto our books, so that we can project strong Net-worth. It is important to gauge financial vitality, like do we have enough cash to take care of any emergencies, do we have enough savings and so on.

We need to evaluate our performance all the time using different financial models and various financial ratios such as:

- Liquidity ratio
- Debt Ratio
- Savings ratio
- Net worth Ratio
- Primary Income Ratio

- Return on capital employed
- Return on net worth
- Replacement costs

Let's analyse each of them in a little more detail:

Liquidity Ratio

This vital sign helps you to assess the extent of safety net that the individual possesses to withstand an economic emergency. In today's uncertain world, where pandemics, economic downturns, medical emergencies and financial catastrophes are a reality; having a large safety net is not only good for your financial health but also for your mental health.

Formula: Liquidity Ratio = Emergency Corpus / Monthly Expenses.

Illustration: Let's say your monthly expenses are 50,000 and your emergency corpus is 10,00,000 then your liquidity ratio is 10,00,000 / 50,000 = 20.

Debt Ratio

This ratio helps you assess the quantum of debt servicing burden the individual is carrying. A high Debt Ratio reflects poorly on their financial health.

Formula: Debt ratio = (Sum of all loan EMI / Monthly Gross salary) * 100

Illustration: Say, you have a home loan EMI of Rs 20,000 and a car loan EMI of Rs 10,000. Your gross monthly earnings is Rs 3 lakh. Then, your debt ratio is 30,000 / 3,00,000 or 10 percent.

Savings ratio

This ratio reflects the savings rate of the individual as a percentage of gross income earned. Many times, folks who end up with a bigger retirement corpus are not necessarily higher earners but bigger savers.

Formula: Savings Ratio= [[Gross monthly savings1 / Gross monthly income] * 100]

Savings includes all statutory deductions

Illustration: Assuming you earn a gross salary of Rs 3 lakh with monthly savings of Rs 60,000, then your savings ratio = [(60,000/3,00,000) X 100] = 20 percent.

Net worth (Adequacy) Ratio

This ratio helps one to assess the financial net worth of an individual considering their income and age.

Formula: Net worth (Adequacy) Ratio = [{Actual Net worth / Expected Net worth} * 100]

Where, actual net worth = Assets – Liabilities

Expected Net worth = 10% X Age X Gross Annual Income (Pre-tax)

Assets include the sum of all your assets like home, car, shares, bonds, surrender value of insurance policies, cash and bank balance, fixed deposits, gold etc., while liabilities is the total of all your loans like home loan / car loan / education loan.

Illustration:

If the total assets of an individual are Rs 80 lakh and the sum of his liabilities is Rs 20 lakh, then actual net worth = (Rs 80 lakh less Rs 20 lakh) = Rs 60 lakh. We have assumed here that the individual is 40 years old, with an annual income of Rs 25 lakh.

The expected net worth = 10% X 40 X 25 lakh = Rs 100 lakh.

Net worth (Adequacy) ratio = [{60 lacs / 100 lacs} * 100] = 60 percent.

Primary Income Ratio

Lastly it is very important to have multiple diverse streams of revenue. It is highly risky to depend on a single source of income as any loss of primary income will significantly affect your financial standing.

Multiple sources can include income from property (rentals), income from investments (dividend / interest, capital gains) and income from royalty among others. One should strive to ensure that one's primary source of income (salary or business) does not exceed 80 percent of total income.

Formula: Primary Income Ratio = [[Primary income / Total Income] * 100

Illustration: Let's say your total income is Rs 30 lakh and the income from your primary source salary is Rs 28 lakh.

Then, your Primary Income Ratio = [[28,00,000 / 30,00,000] X 100] = 93%

Return on Capital Employed

The term return on capital employed (ROCE) refers to a financial ratio that can be used to assess a company's profitability and capital efficiency. In other words, this ratio can help to understand how well a company is generating profits from its capital as it is put to use. Return on capital employed is calculated by dividing net operating profit, or earnings before interest and taxes, by capital employed. Another way to calculate it is by dividing earnings before interest and taxes by the difference between total assets and current liabilities.

Return on Net worth

NET WORTH FORMULA: – **SHAREHOLDER'S EQUITY + RESERVES + PREFERENCE SHARE CAPITAL- MISCELLANEOUS EXPENSES**. A lower ratio indicates that the company is not using the shareholder's fund in growing the business thus decreasing the creditworthiness of the company. The net worth ratio states the return that shareholders could receive on their investment in a company, if all of the profit earned were to be passed through directly to them. Thus, the ratio is developed from the perspective of the shareholder, not the company, and is used to analyse investor returns.

Replacement Cost

Replacement cost refers to the price that it would cost to replace an existing asset with a similar asset at the current market price. The asset in question can be a real estate property, investment security, or account receivable.

With the development of the Islamic Banking, products taking hold around the world, we can utilize these innovative Islamically acceptable financial instruments to leap for further growth.

We need to identify our core competency, constantly upgrading our facilities and systems, always applying innovative new ideas, backed by a strong research and development arm and having a very long-term commitment to planning. I think with these qualities inculcated into us we will always grow and never stagnate

These carefully chosen financial vital signs -- liquidity ratio, debt ratio, savings ratio, net worth ratio and primary income ratio etc. –provide you with a quickly and clearly measurable framework to assess your overall financial health.

An action plan to get these key vital financial signs is a good starting point. A focused, dedicated and well-thought-out plan to increase your liquidity corpus, reduce your loans, increase your savings ratio, grow your net worth and diversify your income sources will ultimately only be beneficial to you.

CASE STUDY:

Business Principles of Abdul Rahman bin Auf (The Companion of Prophet) which earned him 13,188 tons of Gold*

Here we are going to discuss the story of a successful business, wealth, and charity of Abdul Rahman Bin 'Auf (R.A) A very Revered companion of Prophet.

He was one of the very early people who accepted Islam. He is one of those ten people whose entry to paradise was told by Prophet Muhammad (Blessing and Peace be upon Him). When he died, his wealth valued in Gold Coins was three billion one hundred three million Islamic Dinars (3,103,000,000 – 4.25 gms gold per coin).

If the whole wealth is converted into USD then the calculation is approximately more than $501 billion dollars.

Hazrat Abdul Rahman bin Auf was 6 times richer than the Bill Gates. So how he started his business? Let me tell you. His privileged background was common knowledge as he was the son of a successful businessman, 'Auf Bin 'Abd 'Awf.

He was known as a business sensation; his father saw his abilities early when he had taken him out for his business conferences. It didn't take much time that he became the most successful entrepreneur of his time.

When Abdul Rahman (RA) arrived in Medina after migration, he had left all his wealth back in Makkah and he had no money at all, so he had to start from the beginning or we could say that start from scratch. In 622 AD, almost 70 Muslims migrated to Medina with their families.

It was a summer season. In Madina, they stayed with the Ansar (a native of Medina) in their houses, until they could arrange for their own homes. Abdul Rahman (RA) was paired up with Sa'ad Bin Ar-Rabi'ah (RA). He was one of the well-off men of Medina.

At that time, Sa'ad (RA), with big-heartedness and kindness towards his new brother, told Abdul Rahman (RA), "Dear brother, I have the most money among the people of Medina. I have two farms. See which farm you like, I shall empty it for you." Or rather gift it to you

It is the generous example of love that Muslims had for each other. Sa'ad Bin Ar-Rabi'ah was ready to give his wealth and family for the happiness of Allah and offer it to his Muslim brother. Many of the Muslims accepted the division offered to them from their Muslim brothers of Medina, but the response of Abdul Rahman's (RA) was quite impressive.

It is going to give you Goosebumps and you will truly appreciate and respect the will and courage of him. Abdul Rahman (RA) answered to Sa'ad Bin Ar-Rabi'ah (RA) by showing great gratitude, "May Allah bless you with your family and money but just show me the way where the market is." He was talking about "The market of Qainuqa".

He did not wish to become a burden on anyone. During this sadness, there was one optimistic point which was a sign of things to come. **He**

always followed the principle to not to take a loan or gift from anyone because he had a firm belief that Allah (SWT) would provide him, and he had trust in his ability that he could earn in the open market by finding opportunities.

He was a skilled businessman, trained by his father. Before accepting Islam, he was one of the lucky young men of Makkah who was born with silver spoons. He had so much experience that he can smell opportunities and see them everywhere. His passion for seeking opportunities has allowed him to enter the market, use his business wisdom and get benefits from opportunities.

After entering the market, which businesses did Abdul Rahman start with?

He started his trading in a very modest and self-effacing way but he was sharp in scaling the chances he found to convert them into an excellent career of trade progress. Abdul Rahman had started his business by selling some yogurt (dried buttermilk), Oil and butter.

The initial capital of his business was 2 or 4 dinars. Soon he quickly found that horse trading had a good scope in the market, that was his foresightedness and skill, so he started to trade the horses, he realized that profit ratio in this business very small due to great and increasing supply and demand.

He expanded his business soon so he started to sell the saddles also for the horses, that was backward integration which he followed, which was very much money-making business as compared to sell horses. As he bought and traded different commodities, saddles, and horses, due to the volume he turned over, his earnings raised rapidly. Thus, ventured into multiple products.

The brighter future turns into a reality when there are cleanliness and purity in your heart, you are doing your trade with honesty and you know how to measure or scale rightly. From day one when Abdul Rahman (RA) began his own business in the market of Qainuqa in Madina, Allah (SWT) blessed him with reward beyond his expectations.

Later Abdul Rahman became so familiar to business success that he said if he picked up a stone he probably expected to find ornament gold or silver under it! His wealth touched several various businesses. Trade was his profession but he also had agricultural farms besides his business.

Camels were the main source for transportation at that time, and for import and export, you would need them. Initially, he took camels from others. Then he bought his own camels to save the expense of transportation and having his own agricultural land and farms can be a source to feed these camels. Thus, ventured into Logistics looking to his business requirements.

Essential business principles of Hazrat Abdul Rahman Bin Auf (R.A) were very simple

1-The first principle of his business is cash. He always bought goods on cash and sold on cash, no credit deals.

2-Never wait for the higher profit or never stock things. He always tried to avoid storage of goods, he sold goods even if he was offered with one penny of profit. It derived a High level of flow of money, so the main emphasis was on making earnings by increasing profits with a very strong Cash Flow Management.

3-He always made fair deals. He never used to hide any fault in his products. If his product was not up to the mark or if there was even a slight fault in his product, He mentioned it in front of his custom

V

Ethical ... Re- Invent Corporate Governance

Governance is the notions, process, rules and values- constructed within its own socio-political context, gearing organisations to effectively protect and promote its objectives.

The 3C's of Ethical Governance:

- **Constitution**: Outlining the internal management of a company. It also governs the rules of the relationship between management and Stake holders

- **Consent**: It's the acceptance or comprehension of the third component of a business agreement, no matter how you put it, consent makes us better marketers and gives us more success. It makes us Ethical marketers who not only abide by legal situation, but also understand that by being Ethical we're more likely to succeed.

Certainly, was Allah pleased with the believers when they pledge allegiance to you, [O Muhammad], under the tree, and He knew what was in their hearts, so He sent down tranquillity upon them and rewarded them with an imminent conquest *[Quran 48:18]*

- **Consultation:** Here consultation means group decision-making process in which participants develop and decide on proposals with aim or requirement of acceptance by all. Instead of simply voting for an item and having majority of the group getting their way Islam has defined this as Shura

...and consult them in affairs (of moment). Then, when thou hast taken a decision put thy trust in Allah. [Quran 3:159]

[righteous are those] ...who conduct their affairs through [shura baynahum] mutual Consultation. [Quran 42:38]

Principles of Consultation -

1. Members are experts in their field, experienced and knowledgeable
2. Members are free to give their honest opinion without fear or compulsion
3. The final decisions is made by the chairperson in consideration to the opinions of the members *(Either Consultative and Consensus based)*
4. All members must support the final decision made as if it was their own

Ground Rules for a Consultation Meeting

§ One Person speaks at a time and identifies the issues that are important for him or her to discuss as well as what he or she views the conflict to be.

§ Each person should also be prepared with some ideas for solutions to the problem.

§ Listen to what others say about the situation as well as how they felt about it and what they thought about it.

§ If you have something you feel you must say, make a note and wait your turn.

§ PLEASE DON'T INTERRUPT. Each person has a right to be heard completely. You will get your turn.

§ Work hard to understand what the other person is saying even if you need to take notes.

§ Remember that when we are very emotional, our IQ can temporarily drop 10 to 20 points, so be aware that you may be misunderstanding something if you are extremely emotional about the conflict.

§ Be prepared to explain the other person's point of view if you were asked to.

§ Be prepared to explain your feelings, thoughts and needs.

§ Be prepared to try to understand the other person's feelings, thoughts and needs.

§ Be prepared to try to understand the other person's feelings, thoughts and needs both now and in relation to any previous interchange you may be discussing.

§ Be prepared to consider that you may have been mistaken about something, have been missing information, or may have made an incorrect assumption.

§ Follow the instructions of the facilitator/ mediator

§ Be aware of time limits

§ Be willing to make some adjustments in your behaviour if any are requested.

§ Be ready to request behavioural changes from the other person

Corporates worldwide are now reeling from a new wave of 'Shareholders activism'. There is a need to restore shareholder's confidence and increase transparency in Corporate Governance. It is the right time for each of the companies whether a multinational or a regional player to seriously chart out the ways to improve Corporate Governance.

The three Pillars of corporate governance are:

Transparency
Accountability and
Security.

All three are critical in successfully running a company and forming solid professional relationship among its stake holders

Directors can no longer act passively. They need to be alert, responsible and active. These Directors are the leaders of the company and they have to be Humble, Accountable, and Equitable. The regulatory authorities are introducing new compliance and reporting requirements to enhance 'Corporate Governance'

The objective is to help build an environment of Trust, Transparency and accountability necessary to promote long term investments, financial stability and business integrity. Truthfulness is synonymous with fulfilling the trust, and lying is equivalent to Treachery.

The regulators worldwide are working on identifying the sound practices which are necessary to strengthen the resilience of critical financial markets in the face of scandals in corporate world. The Securities Exchange Board of India (SEBI) has issued a statement regarding 'Management's Discussion and Analysis of Financial Condition and Results of Operations'; which suggests steps that companies should consider on meeting their disclosure obligations. The disclosure matters addressed are liquidity and capital resources including off-balance sheet arrangements; certain trading activities that include non-exchange traded contracts accounted at fair value; and effect of transactions with related and certain other parties.

The Core fundamental for Governance:

- Ethical Business Practice: A code of Conduct is central theme for a successful corporate business strategy and thereby define a company's business practices
- Aligning Company goals with Governance: Planning and framing the organisation's goal and to align them with the goals assigned by their governance programme which lightens up the burden of company's leaders.
- Management strategy: Rights of Minority stakeholders. This is the protection which the Management and Board of Directors should grant to the minority stakeholders of their rights. Management should maintain Pluralism, Tolerance, Freedom, Openness and Broadmindedness in their approach towards various stake holders, employees and affiliates of the company

In recent times, Corporate Governance has emerged as a widely acclaimed conclusive niche for corporate success. Corporate Governance is vital to enable companies to compete globally in a sustained manner and to make them flourish. I t leads to higher degree of corporate excellence wherefrom enhanced success emanates yielding long-term value additions to the stakeholders. Corporate Governance is not merely about enacting legislations but about establishing a climate of trust, confidence and creativity among various constituents. Strengthening Corporate Governance is fundamentally an ongoing process in which the Government, Corporate Sector and professionals have to synergise. Corporate dedicated towards enhancing stakeholder value need to adopt highest standards of transparency, accountability professionalism, social responsiveness and ethical business practices as a self-disciplining code for corporate Governance. Good Corporate Governance entails making a corporate a responsible corporate citizen that will not only augment the stakeholder wealth but also contribute towards social good.

I firmly believe that Corporate Governance is the application of best management practices, compliance of law in true letter and spirit and adherence to ethical standards for effective management and distribution of wealth and discharge of social responsibility for sustainable development of all stakeholders. Companies will need to begin developing strategic plans to guide better the transition of certain powers and reflect the growing control and importance of the stakeholders.

A solid Organisational structure is essential for smooth implementation and dispersing corporate governance objectives. Companies need to monitor all of their dealings, interaction, and transactions effectively. A very core objective is to develop more transparent business practices, a rigidly structured framework through which one can trace all such activities efficiently.

Fraud and Risk Management a very critical topic to be taken into consideration when implementing a compliance strategy so as to prevent any unlawful or illicit activity

The Corporate Governance can be segregated on to the following areas:

1. **Board Members: Roles and Responsibilities**

There should be a shared understanding and agreement about key roles and responsibilities of Directors 'individually' and the Board as a 'whole'. Internationally best practices should be adopted and key indicators on characteristics of a 'high performing Boards' should be identified. Steps should be undertaken to reduce conflict of interest

1. **Role of the Board of Members in Selecting the Chief Executive Officer**

The role of the Board of members in setting goals for the CEO should be properly identified. Criteria should be evaluated for selection of the CEO. Most important responsibility of the Board is to have the best possible CEO. It can also be the most challenging task. Forward looking questions should be generated that address ways the CEO can take the organisation in the desired future. The selection of Key Managerial positions and other Office Bearers should be as follows

- Capability and Strength
- Trustworthy and Honesty
- Experience and Knowledge
- No Relatives (No Nepotism)
- No officer of company allowed to do personal business (Conflict of Interest)

3. **Strategic Direction**

The business strategy should be reviewed, monitored and ensured that it is implemented. The Board of members should be relentlessly focussed on the strategic direction of the organisation. There should be a balance between strategic focus and operational management. Objectives should be to align the strategy throughout the organisation. A framework should be established for 'Annual Strategy review' that includes scenario planning for the organisation.

4. **Performance of the Board**

Periodic review should be made for the performance of the Board. Corporate reputation and image can be endangered which can have serious consequences. Time, energy, effort, and money are wasted if Board members do not fulfil their duties. A 360-degree Board performance feedback should be obtained which draws on the collective wisdom of 'those who care' about the organisation.

5. **Interpersonal Dynamics**

The CEO, Board members and employees must work together as a 'Team' to achieve common goals. Officials of the organisation must be closely supervised and monitored by the leadership. Their recruitment must be on merit as defined above and a credible accountability mechanism must be in place, otherwise corruption and misrule will reign supreme. Effective communication skills should be identified and established at all levels, level 'team effectiveness' and 'emotional intelligence' should be periodically assessed. On the criteria of Justice its deemed that a proper equation should be maintained between the rights and obligations of employees and various stake holders.

The Directors should acknowledge the importance of the guidelines set out in the principles of Good Governance and the Code of Best Practice published by the Committee on Corporate Governance in June 1998. The Directors intend to implement procedures to ensure that the Company complies with the Combined Code to the extent, which the Directors consider to be appropriate for the size of the company.

The Board should propose to establish the Audit and Remuneration committees, both with formally delegated duties and responsibilities.

- An Audit committee should be establishing when appropriate including Non-Executive Directors. It will be responsible both for ensuring that the financial information of the Company is properly reported on and monitored and for meeting the auditors and reviewing their reports relating to the accounts and internal control systems.
- The Remuneration Committee will review the scale and structure of the Executive Directors remuneration and the terms of their service contracts. The Board will set the remuneration and terms and condition of the appointment of the Non-Executive Directors.
- The Directors recognise that the system of internal controls and reporting procedures is vital and will focus their efforts in implementing such systems as are required to control revenues, costs and quality thresholds at each of company's locations.

- In addition, the Directors have proposed to have fortnightly management meetings and quarterly Board meetings in which a formal agenda covering all aspects of business is followed and that accurate and timely records are maintained as well as timely implementation or fulfilment of agreed actions and measures is consistently achieved.
- To ensure that the financial conducts of the company are at all times compliant with high ethical standards and all relevant statutory, contractual and regulatory requirements are adhered to, the Board has developed and accepted a robust financial management and control procedures.

Chart of Authority: **For detail refer Appendix**

It is basically a segregation of Duties. The company shall delegate to discharge the duties in accordance to the laid down principles and approved by Board of Directors or the competent authority in accordance with Chart of Authority and responsibilities assigned to the departments.

FINANCIAL CONTROL & PROCEDURE: For detail refer Appendix

- **Description and assessment of the key financial systems and internal controls, including financial information supplied to management, estimating and forecasting procedures, cash management and the debtors and creditors control systems.**

MODEL CODE OF CONDUCT: **For detail refer Appendix**

This code of Conduct (hereinafter referred to as the "Code for the Employees and Sr. Officers of the Company) is laid down by the Board of Directors.

The Code is aimed to set out the broad guidelines for the ethical business conduct by the Employees and Senior Officials of the Company and ensure compliance with the requirements specifically under the revised management policy with an underlying objective to discourage wrong practice and promote ethical conduct of the business of the Company.

The Code is formulated in line with the interest of all the stakeholders of the Company namely, the shareholders, business partners and employees of the Company.

The Code is applicable to the following persons, referred to as "Officers".

1. All the employees on the payroll of the Company;
2. All Functional heads and persons above that level.

VI
Family Business

As the name suggests a family-owned corporation is a business owned primarily or exclusively by family members. As business grows, it can be challenging to run the business using only family members.

Ho Aasmaan sii Manzil
Ya Samandar sa Raasta
Bas Ek Uthe Qadam se
Tay Hota hai ye Faasla

Translation: Yes, sky is the destination
or road like an Ocean
just with one step
The distance is determined

Success comes to those who stay focused and never give up on their goals...!!!! Just as Life is a series of baby steps.... first generation entrepreneurs' family business venture is a small step in a right direction, which can turn out to be the biggest step of an entrepreneur's life. Don't let the fear of Failure or rejection hold you back from your dream. Your future is your responsibility. Nobody else can do it for you. Your heart knows exactly what the mind wants. Once you take that first step you will never look back.

Don't be disheartened or depressed by dreams not going your way. Hard times, tough times, rough times, anxious times, stressful times, don't last long, have faith in your abilities and faith in God, he will never let u down...

Himmat e Marda........ tu Madad e Khuda (God always favors the brave)

A good recipe for a successful business families:

- **Trust**:

Most successful business run on the basics of trust and honesty. It is typically the biggest determinant in success. The relationship of family members is based on trust. This makes the business running since problems within finance, management or supervision won't be witnessed.

- **Vision:**

Every member of a family has a purpose and a vision to make business successful. Their primary aim is that business runs from one generation to another, hence they have laid out plan to achieve the vision of the company. Moreover, a full proof succession plan is in place. They work on developing the next team of business leaders. Also, it is ascertained that everyone aligns with the values and vision of the family.

Be thankful for what you have...Be creative, innovative. Think differently and positively. Face your past without regrets, handle your present with confidence. Prepare for the future without fear. Keep the faith and drop the fear.

- **Unity:**

Families are brought together due to their unity. Each member of the family places the interest of business ahead of their self-interest. Due to the unity communication and decision making becomes less complex. Every member gets a chance to contribute to their views and ideas and this is possible when all members are on same page of their vision and goals.

To maintain unity, it's important to convene frequent family meetings to clear misunderstandings if any and to educate other members about the business. And more important it builds a conflict resolution skills and also generates the qualities of effective and efficient communication skills.

- **<u>Positive and ethical values</u>**:

Family ethics are usually based on the foundation of the family. This foundation gives a positive thinking among its members which helps individuals to produce rational and positive thinking thought process for serving their fellow employees and customers. Studies have indicated that 85%of family businesses are run by ethical standards and family values. It's not all about money, most family businesses work towards providing an economic opportunity to the community particularly in terms of employment.

- **<u>Ability to take risks and losses</u>:**

Family business are more used to taking calculated risk by diversifying business more than others. This allows them to leverage existing knowledge to grow. Though they expand to business within the same or related industries by going either backward or forward integration.

Self-Belief is the key word for taking calculated risks in business.

Believe in yourself, in the power you have....
To control your business and its life, day by day
Believe in the strength, that you have deep inside
And your faith will help show you the way
Believe inn tomorrow, and it will bring success
Let in hopeful heart carry on through your business journey
For things will work out, if you TRUST and BELIEVE
For there's no limit what you can do......As....
THE SKY'S THE LIMIT

The unity of the elder members of the family with their younger generation a generation next helps the family business to adapt well to technological and other change even though maintain their traditional environment. Though they might not be the just users of technology but are quick to respond. This is primarily because the elders focus on the next generation and the younger family members have the ear of leadership. The elders are unable to cope up with the techniques of digitalization and various other trends which are emerging now-a-days.

A family enterprise always goes through some testing times……but whenever there is a choice…choose UNITY, AND LOVE above Mistrust and Misunderstanding, choose KINDNNESS and COMPASSION with fellow members and employees above anger and resentment choose SELFLESSNESS above selfishness, with an attitude of forgive…. Forgive yourself, forgive others and Forgive everyone, as everybody is working for the success of a business enterprise. Be compassionate to yourself and be compassionate to others

My grandfather used to always say- "That if my employee makes a loss it is a loss, but if I make a loss it's an experience".

This above axiom gives lot of boost for a family member to take calculated risk for the betterment of an organization.

CHALLENGES: -

The true spirit of a businessman is to face the challenges in a sporting way. Take the bull by its horn. As all businesses face challenge same holds true for a family business. The same old challenges of changing Economy, or getting the right mix of employees. Whether it is increased competition or changing government policies, family businesses are not immune to these challenges.

STRUGGLE……will Exhausts you, irritates you and sometimes Demoralize you. But it gives you the elegant reward of life time called SUCCESS

But there are certain unique challenges, Issues the family enterprise faces.

Emotions: In a certain ways family business is more driven by emotions rather than financial strategy for longer sustainability. Family issues play more important role in the decision making of strategic business issues, which ultimately creates difficult political situation for family members.

The founder works and build a business, the son inherits but is ill equipped to manage and make it grow, but enjoys the wealth......and the generation Next inherits a business which is already on its way to be dead. Faith is the soul of success. The people who accomplish the most do so not because they never run into problem, but because they believe there is a solution for everyone.

Remember we should not indulge in Blame Game Politics. Believe that a Good person gives Happiness, Bad person gives experience, and a worst person teaches us a lesson.

Lack of Vision: These emotions lead to absence of clear policies and business norms among the family, and who is reluctant to have outside opinions and advises and also lack of courage and diversity on how to operate a business. No business plans in place or documented, neither have any long-term planning. They lack vision and knowledge of their own business and its worth, and the factors that make it valuable or unvaluable. They lack vision for the further growth of the company by infusing capital by way of new investment and resist to re-invest in the business. Ultimately this leads to different vision and different goals by each family member. It's important to Dream Big because as you dream, so shall you become.... YOUR vision is the promise of what you shall one day be; Your ideal is the prophecy of what you shall at last unveil.

Man Power: Non-Qualified family members by virtue of succession comes into key Roles and responsibility. These members are not qualified and having lack of skills and abilities for the organization. These makes the employees of the company highly insecure, resulting in high attrition level of the good, skilled non-family employees. Hence a proper training of the family members is required to integrate them in the organization. They should be trained to provide them specific information about their goals, expectations and obligations of the position they enjoy by virtue of being a family member. Control of the organization should hence be not influenced by tradition but a good management practices should be followed, so that control of operations does not become difficult for members of the family. A proper involvement of each member of family is required in day to day of work and supervision.

THE ROAD TO SUCCESSFUL FAMILY BUSINESS:

CONSENSUS APPROACH/ UNITY: Each member in a family is secured in his position, ideas take shape quickly due to its family staff able to take risks. Avoid playing with emotions, by giving a family member a role he is not ready for, or rather putting a family member into a position he is not able to do justice and which ultimately hinder the performance of the business. If a right person for the right position can't be found among family members, its better to bring from outside who has the required skills.

अकेले हम बूँद हैं,
मिलि जाएं तो सागर हौं
अकेले हम धागा हैं,
मिलि जाएं तो चादर हौं
अकेले हम कागज हैं,
मिलि जाएं तो किताब हौं
जीवन का आनन्द मिलिजुल कर रहने में ही है

Translation: Alone we are drops,
If together, they are the ocean.
Alone we are the thread,
If together, it is a sheet.
Alone we are paper,
If bind together, it is a book.
the joy of life is in living together

One very important aspect of Consensus approach is to have In place a very good corporate Governance. I am doing a detailed chapter on Corporate Governance for its better understanding. A good governance can have a family constitution. This constitution needs to work on consensus decision for some tough decisions which can ultimately build cohesion and internal harmony, creation of strong business ethical guidelines. Its important to have a very strong code of Conduct which further establishes the rules around conflict.

The most important Rule for Consensus Approach is the ability to LISTEN & PATIENCE. This comes with major difference of opinion between founder's belief and young members enthusiasm. The downfall of family business is if the older generations do not listen to younger ones.

Yes, Old is Gold....... the older family believe in tried and tasted ways of doing, but the younger lot have innovative ideas of improving things.

SUCCESSION/CONTINUITY IN BUSINESS: Yes, one major family business failure is lack of succession plan.

According to Family business survey report of KPMG, 17% FAMILY OWNED BUSINESS HAVE DOCUMENTED PLANS FOR THE FUTURE OF BUSINESS. Succession is not something that can be achieved overnight. Have people from non-family as your core team for making a good succession roadmap. They will bring much needed outside perspective and not let family issues influence their decision. Its important to have consensus approach among all stakeholders for endorsing the succession plans.

To avoid family conflicts, poor leadership decision and loss of vision, which inevitably leads to the fall of a business, a proper well-defined succession plan should be in place, which also becomes a guiding light for the incoming leader which helps him in managing the company and putting the leaders vision and future direction on the right path.

VII

MSME: THE GATEWAY FOR A SUCCESSFUL ENTREPRENEURSHIP

Let's start our topic of how to Create a MSME Business in a Ethical way. There are the 3 keys for Ethical Business practice.

- The Trustworthy
- Truthfulness
- Fulfil Promise and Trust

Prophet (SAW) Was known as Al-Amin or The Trustworthy. He earned this title based on his reputation as a successful Merchant.

Prophet (SAW) Said, Speak the Truth & always keep your promises & fulfil your trust. And truthfulness is the foundation of all human virtues. These 3 are Main ingredients of the successful Business

So, Let`s Start and do our Business by setting up MSME in an Ethical Way.

My word of Encouragement to lot of young Entrepreneur.

I would say:

Sahas aur Himmat, Zindagi mein Bahut zaruri hai. (Courage and Daring is very Important in Life)

Courage is the willingness to act inspite of fear.

Feel Empathy it is the caring & sharing attitude with our employee

Have Faith in Technology & Talent

Always adopt to change with time.......... and

last heart to heart Relation with our Business that is called passion or Dil ka Rishta.

So, let's PLAN out our Work & Start Working on our Plan.

Mein Aadat hu uski Woh Zarurat hai meri

Mein farmaish hu uski woh Ibadat hai Meri.

Itni Aasaani se kaise nikal du usey is dil se

woh khawaab hai mera, main Haqiqat hu uski

Summarised Translation of Urdu couplet

Make your business your habit, and your honesty will make your business your religion/ritual, which will fulfil your wishes. Hence it will be imbedded in your passion to fulfil all your dream into reality.

<u>Introduction:</u>

MSME stands for Micro, Small and Medium Enterprise. In accordance with the Micro, Small, and Medium Enterprises Development (MSMED) Act. In 2006, these enterprises are classified into two divisions—Manufacturing enterprise, and Service enterprise:

The MSME sector is the backbone of the Indian Economy, since MSME PRODUCE AND MANUFACTURE VARIETY OF PRODUCTS FOR BOTH DOMESTIC AS WELL AS international markets, they help promote the growth and development of various product segments and industries. Further MSME play an important role in generating employment opportunities. It helps in the industrialization of backward and underprivileged areas.

Recently in June 2020 GOI have redefined MSME'S in terms of its level of Investment & Turnover. So, that more & more companies can avail maximum benefit of Govt. Subsidies & Sops. The investment and turnover figures were changed to larger values, there by resulting in more numbers of medium sized enterprises can be benefited out of it.

THE NEW CLASSIFICATION:

- Micro: Where level of Investment <Rs. 1 Crore & Annual Turnover < Rs. 5 Crore.

- Small: Where level of Investment < Rs 10 Crore & Annual Turnover < Rs 50 Crore.

- Medium: Where level of investment < Rs 50 Crore & Annual Turnover <Rs. 250 Crore.

Looking to the classification we as Entrepreneurs can take lot of benefits from Govt. Schemes which are not always Interest based, or fund based schemes but also are in form of subsidies, and Tax holidays etc.

These could be the major industries in MSME Segment

- Agriculture product
- Food Processing
- Chemical & Dyestuff
- Pharmaceuticals & Medical Equipment
- Electricals & Electronics
- Textile
- Meat Product
- Plastics
- Computer Software/ Hardware

MSME'S through their various business ventures enable citizen to venture out on their own and in turn give back to society by creating new jobs, they have also steadily revived artisan class in remote areas of the country by providing opportunities of showcasing their talents and converting into employment avenues. The MSME's are always inn support of technology and its upgradation, infrastructure development which helps in modernization of country and society as a whole.

Basic Overview of MSME In India

- Total Registered MSME`s 51 Million
- Contribution to total Manufacturing output 45 %
- Contribution to Exports 50 %
- Total Industrial Enterprises 80 %
- Contribution to GDP 20 %

- MSME is the growth engine across the world
- All big Industries depend on its survival on MSME`s in India
- These MSME`s has made India to become one of the fastest growing Economies

This is the contribution of MSME's in India's Growth Story. Total Registered MSME's is 51 Million. And in terms of absolute numbers MSME's contribute a staggering 30% to the country's GDP and around 45% of the manufacturing output and approximately 45% of the country's exports. MSME has created 11 Crore Jobs opportunities in India and employing 40% of Indian Workforce. This is the reason it's the backbone of India's economic development and the reason why they are so crucial to be supported. Now with the pandemic gradually and slowly waning and economic activity is slowly coming back to life, it becomes more sense for business owners to get their MSME Registration done and avail a wide array of benefits. Though Registration which are optional and If you are not registered as MSME then you are losing the opportunity from getting advantages of Govt. Schemes.

Challenges of Being MSME:

1. **Operational Challenge**
2. **Cultural Challenge**

Operational Challenge:

- Liquidity
- Marketing and Sales
- Labour/ Manpower
- Raw material

Liquidity
is the first and foremost challenge MSME's are facing. It's very important to conserve Cash → how to conserve, we need to negotiate with our creditors for extended credit periods, getting Discount in Purchase, we need to be strong on receivables & improve our collections process. Try to explore for alternates - Never store all eggs in one basket. Cash Conversation is Critical and a key to Success. And Positive working Capital generally indicates the health of an Enterprise.

Marketing & Sales

- Support your existing customers immediate needs in terms of Pricing & Products & Re priotise their needs

- Shift to safe & secure and cheap form of communications/ Marketing i.e. Digital
- Scan the competitive landscape to spot opportunities
- Explore value additions to product e.g. accreditation, alliances, of new inputs in products

Labour /Man Power

- You need to align the team to organizational Goal
- Regular interactions between Team members & arranging their Training needs
- Share business updates to employees & constant communication has to be kept with Employees
- Encourage Employees having right attitude – through open house meet
- Organize Events to have bonding between employees & various teams

Cultural Challenge:

- Traditional Business Setups through inheritance/or Succession
- Unprofessional Approach towards Running a business
- Running the enterprise in a Bureaucratic Manner and lack of Management skills
- Totally engage in Administrative Roles

We are in a setup of traditional Business where accruing a technology & maintaining competitiveness is a big challenge.

Unprofessional attitude & bureaucratic approach towards our human Resources. We do not generally match wages as per Industry norms, so Job security is at stake for the employees. And because we do not match wages, our enterprise becomes a training ground and attrition level is very high, hence we lack skilled labor and competent manpower.

We become Jack of all Trade & Master of none by handling all day to day basic Administrative hassles of Organization. Because of Too many administrative roles we have little chance to think of growth, innovation which is essentially required for Growth.

So we need to improve in our approach towards our own organization, and be creative, Innovative for our success and survival. But the key to our challenges is TO BE ATMANIRBHAR MSME, by accepting its registration and making full use of Government backed schemes and processes.

Underestimating inflation

Almost everyone who is keen on being financially free in 10 years or less but they are unable to estimate effect of Inflation. A good rule of thumb to remember would be that at 7 percent inflation, your expenses will nearly double every 10 years, even when you are conscious of not unnecessarily upgrading your Business.

So, if you're spending X amount today, you will be spending 2X in 10 years, 4X in 20 years, 8X in 30 years and so on. Simply put, because people underestimate the effect of inflation, the actual corpus required for financial freedom is often much in excess of what people estimate it to be.

Getting Registered as a MSME: ADVANTAGE START

In a recent initiative by Government of India, Ministry of MSME to handhold the registered Business entrepreneurs in their venture and providing them encouragement and support along with solving their problems and grievances in taking their business forward have come up with a portal called CHAMPION PORTAL. It's a sort of control room for solving issues online.

What is CHAMPIONS Portal?

It's an acronym which stands for **C**reation & **H**armonious **A**pplication of **M**odern **P**rocess for **I**ncreasing **O**utput & **N**ational **S**cheme

Champions.gov.in is with features like AI Artificial Intelligence, Data Analytics and Machine Learning with fully integrated Real-Time basis grievance portal like CPGrams

So before we try to understand the Benefits of MSME, lets know the process of Registering as MSME

Now to take your objective of being a complete MSME, most important, is the Registration as MSME. All those MSME already registered previously under any scheme or by any Registration Authority under MSME has to re- register under New process called Udhyam Registration which was applicable from 1st July'20.

Who can apply for MSME?

• Proprietorship

- Own- One Person Company
- Limited Liability Partnership (LLP)
- Private Limited company
- Limited Company
- Association of Person
- Co Operative Society

The Benefits of being Registered and Part of MSME growth story are immense and will give a first mover advantage.

The Benefits can be classified as both Tangible & Non-Tangible, Fund Based and Non-Fund based.

So first & foremost you get your Basics under control

- Proof of Legal Existence.
- Marketing support/ Assistance (Bar Code) e g. Assistance will be provided for Participation in exhibition within India for Stall rent etc. Assistance in creating Bar code.
- Reimbursement of Certification/ Accreditation fees for ISO etc. With a Vision to encourage domestic products to be globally competitive and to promote quality certification to obtain ISI/WHO-GMP & ISO.
- Subsidy on Patent Registration
- Credit Rating Support
- Concession in Electric Bills
- Preference in Government Tenders
- International Push
- Protection Against Delayed Payments

These are just a few examples of level of support MSME gets on getting registered.

Though the major benefits of being Registered as MSME's are fund based. And since my vision is Ethical business practice and in an Interest free environment, I will not go into much detail on fund based benefits, as you will find lot of material on fund based financing on the other hand, Interest free financial products (Sharia Compliant Products) are flexible and are also compliant with all applicable Indian laws though in its infancy stage, but its formation is with the vision of fulfilling the requirements of our Ethical MSME's enterprises for providing them Interest (Riba) free financing.

But still, we need to know what the Government is providing us in terms of fund Based financing.

Fund-Based

- Credit Facilities through Banks with Low Interest rate
- Term Loans for Fixed Assets
- Working Capital Requirement
- Exemption of Interest
- Overdraft Facilities
- Priority Sector Lending

Non-Fund Based

- Guarantees
- Letter of Credit
- Foreign Bank Guarantees
- Foreign Letter of Credit

It's the Government's intentions to lift the Spirit of MSME's as it is the backbone of the economy. Government has initiated various programmed for the growth of MSME Sector.

- To Create E-Market linkage for MSME's to act as replacements for Trade fair and Exhibition. E.G GeM
- Technology DRIVEN SYSTEM TO ENHANCE TRANSACTIONS BASED LENDING USING DATA FROM E-MARKET PLACE
- Government will continuously monitor settlement of dues to MSME Vendors from Government and Central PSU's

ATMANIRBHAR BHARAT……. ATMANIRBHAR MSME

Our Honorable PM has coined this beautiful and called AtmaNirbhar Bharat (Self Reliant India)

So, we also want to be AtmaNirbhar – MSME (Self-Reliant Indian MSME)

So, what is AtmaNirbhar its overview & how to be AtmaNirbhar in our Business and what we can achieve by being AtmaNirbhar is the key to our success.

So, let's understand what are the bases and key attributes of being AtmaNirbhar. Establishing the 5 Strengths

- Economy
- Infrastructure
- Technology Driven System
- Demography
- Demand

Objectives of AtmaNirbhar

- Liquidity Infusion
- In Growth and Critical sectors to make them globally competitive and attractive

To infuse Liquidity in our venture as the most Imp Interim Measure. And by infusing Liquidity how to Grow in critical Sectors, to make ourselves globally & locally competitive & attractive.

So, after understanding the objectives, Yes Establish a legal Business Entity with all statutory and optional Registration & create a strong Business/ Project Report /Plan highlighting your Business Model & your Strengths & USP's. Your strong Profile with Moderate & reasonable financials. And this is where we need

"Quick Decision; Backed by Information"

Set your Goals High but Achievable

And Get Going Without Fear and With a Big Smile

1. **<u>Liquidity is</u>** the first and foremost challenge we as MSME's are facing. It's very important to conserve Cash → how to conserve, we need to negotiate with our creditors for extended credit periods, getting Discount in Purchase, we need to be strong on receivables & improve our collections process. Try to explore for alternates - Never store all eggs in one basket. Cash Conversation is Critical and a key to Success. And Positive working Capital generally indicates the health of an Enterprise.

Marketing & Sales

- Support your existing customers immediate needs in terms of Pricing & Products & Repriotize their needs
- Shift to safe & secure and cheap form of communications/ Marketing i.e. Digital
- Scan the competitive landscape to spot opportunities
- Explore value additions to product e.g. accreditation, alliances, of new inputs in products

Labor /Man Power

- You need to align the team to organizational Goal
- Regular interactions between Team members & arranging their Training needs
- Share business updates to employees & constant communication has to be kept with Employees
- Encourage Employees having right attitude – through open house meet

Organize Events to have bonding between employees & various teams

12
HABITS OF HIGHLY PRODUCTIVE PEOPLE

Source : (Internet)

2. We are in a setup of traditional Business where accruing a technology & maintaining competitiveness is a big challenge.

Unprofessional attitude & bureaucratic approach towards our human Resources. We do not generally match wages as per Industry norms, so Job security is at stake for the employees. And because we do not match wages, our enterprise becomes a training ground and attrition level is very high, hence we lack skilled labor and competent manpower.

We become Jack of all Trade & Master of none by handling all day to day basic Administrative hassles of Organization. Because of Too many admin roles we have little chance to think of growth, innovation which is essentially required for Growth.

So we need to improve in our approach towards our own organization, and be creative, Innovative for our success and survival.

3. Mobilization of fund is not a challenge but a bigger challenge is its utilization.

For financing Muslim Business houses, the roadblock is the transparency of our business. We are afraid of losing control of the enterprises, which is not the case.

Sharia Compliant Products are Flexible and it unlocks your capital. You avoid equity dilution, which are compliant with all applicable Indian laws and most important transparent & hassle-free formalities.

VIII

GROWING BUSINESS IN AN INTEREST FREE ENVIRONMENT

As I always say we in India are still in its initial rather infancy stage of developing Interest free financial products, but here I have tried to help readers to fulfil their goals of growing their business in the most ethical and sharia compliant way, This chapter is my, first baby steps to fulfil the vision of entrepreneurs by being their counsellor and mentor between a business owner & his dreams.

Deewarein Unchi Hai, Galiyan Hai Tang
Lambi Dagar Hai Par Himmat Hai Sang
Paaon Pe Chale Hai, Saansein Buland
Ladne Chala Hu Interest se Azadi Ki Jang
Bekhauf Interest Ki Aazadi se Hai Jeena Mujhe!
Bekhauf Aazad Hai Rehna Mujhe!

Translation: The walls are high; the streets are narrow
The road is long but there is courage
Walking on my feet with breath high
I am going to fight the war for freedom from interest
I have to live with the freedom of interest fearlessly

I am free to live without fear

As discussed in my earlier chapters about how Islam had identified the ills of an unjust Interest-based Economic system, not only Islam but practically all major religion in the world, Hinduism, Judaism, or Christianity have their own ills of this unjust system with both ancient and spiritual views of interest.

"Usury was identified as the practice of charging financial gains in excess of the principal amount of the loan taken."

But now the modern definition has been tweaked to look as ethical and acceptable.

"Usury is now interpreted as interest above the legal or socially acceptable rate".

I have dwelled upon the spiritual and religious guidelines both ancient views as well as modern concept in my introductory chapter.

The Quran did not just stop with an injunction on Interest but in the same sentence encouraged enterprise and trade. That Ayat in Surah Al-Imraan spell out

Allah has permitted Trade and forbidden Interest

Let me make it very clear Sharia (Islamic jurisprudence) has never and will never contravenes any Law of any country on the contrary it is complimentary to it. My first and foremost advice to entrepreneurs is to be Transparent in Business operations. For Financing our business or rather maintaining Financial discipline there are many ways and ethical product to support our business, and these products are flexible and which unlocks your capital without diluting your capital. But before going in these detail lets understand Financial discipline our financial system.

Financial Discipline:

It's basically how well we are able to plan and confirm our spending and savings as per our plans we have set to achieve our monetary goals. Without your financial plans its really difficult to be disciplined, to achieve your short term and long-term dreams are your plans, A proper financial discipline reduces the stress level, and you make sure you have the money for the things on which you really want to spend.

- Be Realistic: Set realistic goals, as it will make you feel capable of achieving your goals. Your thought process should be on track for spending on things which add value to your business.
- Budgeting: Focus on your plans will help in setting budget. So, prior to budgeting have a clear picture of what you are dealing with and also need to evaluate your income in terms of your priorities.
- Set Goals: You need to have clear vision of your goals and make a practical and achievable plan. Its most crucial part of financial discipline.
- Mindful Spending: Another crucial aspect of financial discipline is your spending, its where and how you spend the hard-earned money.
- Mindful Saving: Your future lies in your actions of today. So when you start thinking for future you are mature enough to think of proper saving for something that actually matters and part of your future plans. And to save you need constant motivation since changing your lifestyle can be hard enough than what you might think of.
- Motivation: Keep motivating yourself, challenge yourself to stick to your goals and to your allocated budget. Motivate yourself to discipline your finances by changing your environment

Practicing financial discipline is not a one-time thing. You need to follow your plan despite the constant peer pressure. Have a NEVER GIVE UP ATITTUDE

We need to identify our core competency, constantly upgrading our facilities and systems, always applying innovative new ideas, backed by a strong research and development arm and having a very long-term commitment to planning. I think with these qualities inculcated into us we will always grow and never stagnate.

Financial System:

The Indian Financial system enables lenders and borrowers to exchange funds, which is controlled by Independent Regulators in the sector of Insurance, Banking, Capital Markets and various other service sectors. This financial system accelerates the rate and volume of savings through the provision of various financial instruments and efficient mobilization of savings. This financial system then helps efficiently direct the flow of savings and investments in the economy. These savings are then channelized by banks to provide credit to different business entities which are involved in production and distribution.

So, let's understand this financial system in an Islamic perspective

Regulators	Conventional	Islamic
Banks/NBFC's	Interest based	Interest free
Capital Markets	Bonds Financial Screening	Equity Business screening
Insurance	Trading of Risk Conflict of Interest	Sharing of Risk Solidarity & Mutuality
Fund based instruments	Collateral mortgage, Overdraft facilities Credit facility	Mudarbaha (Profit sharing & loss bearing) Musharka (Joint Venture) Murabaha (cost-plus) Ijara (Leasing)

As seen in above table Islamic financial system encompasses the Islamic Banking system, Islamic Money/ Capital Market, Islamic Insurance (Takaful) which provides alternate sources of financing

Islamic finance addresses the issue of Financial Inclusion and gives access to finance from 2 directions.

1. Promoting Risk sharing contracts a very viable alternative to conventional debt based financing.
2. Specific customised instruments of redistribution of wealth among the society.

Now we have fully understood Financial system both conventional, and Islamic along with Financial discipline, lets understand the need of finance. It's a part of business which is responsible for managing money within organisation, this includes acquiring funds, managing the finances of the business, and planning future expenditure.

Businesses can face monetary constraints due to shortage of funds, finance is the main fuel of every business, no matter what size in such a scenario taking loan can help power up the enterprise

FINANCIAL OBSTACLES FOR MSME's:

- Observed that Small & Medium Enterprise faces obstacles to access capital.

- SME's, bank on their own capital & unorganized borrowing

- Poor Access to Large Financial Institute (now BSE has started SME Exchange)

But the reality of life for an Entrepreneur and the primarily reason in SME's or as a matter of fact MSME's is they do face difficulties to get finance. Reason is that their universe is diverse & scale of economies is small. The Financial Institution typically target process driven and look for scalable opportunities. Secondly due to poor company Information & weak control and rather no corporate governance it's difficult to assess and analyses the operation of MSME's. The financial institutions are not equipped to address low return on their efforts as the MSME's lack management Resources & Capital Bandwidth.

Hence now suppose in such worst-case scenario, if we have to go for further infusion of fund ------ Then what?

So, there are 2 ways, Interest or Interest free. It could be borrowed capital what we call LOAN, which could be either interest based or Interest-free. Or it could be any form of equity participation on sharia principles or pure equity through stock exchange route.

So First let us study Interest. I know, most of you know it, but let me go according to major Religion of the world prevailing at the times.

As discussed earlier, not a single major religion allows Interest.......In Ancient Hinduism, 400 BC vasishtha, an ancient Hindu law maker forbade, interest taking by higher castes Brahmans & Kshatriyas, similarly, Judaism has its roots in biblical passage of forbidding & discouraging of taking interest.

Same with Christianity right from 5th century AD to 8th century Ad till as early 1311, Popes made ban on usury way absolute & declared all legislation in its favour null & void. And for Islam we all know it is well established in the Holy Quran.

Now it becomes very important for us to know what is Interest and what is Interest-free

Interest: -

It was defined as a practice of charging financial extra in excess of the principal amount of Loan, further it got more evolved with the greed of the lenders & made it more cancerous for the society. It is that form of Interest which is above the legal or socially acceptable rate. This is usually charged by the private lenders in unorganised market. E.g. Opportunity cost, Interest on Interest etc.,

Interest–Free: -

A financial practice that draws inspiration from Quran that prohibits interest & harmful practices. It accounts for moral consequences of financial Transaction & ensure it is fair & equitable to all parties in terms of risk effort able & responsibility borne by all parties.

BORROWED FUNDS HARMFUL TO BUSINESS:

- According to financial Analyst High Debt to Equity Ratio is a sign of weak Business.

- Debt is addictive ------A trap in debt spiral

- A Bad Vicious Circle

ALTERNATE: INTEREST FREE BUSINESS AND ITS PURPOSE; -

- Sharia finance as it is called, is an Asset Based & Need Based economy.

- It creates a perfect foundation for a just and ethical business practice.

- It creates a habit of sharing & caring between an owner & its Investor.

- By regular Audits for checking Business, harmful & Un-Islamic activities, it also gets checked of its financial flaws.

The decision to go for debt alters the course & condition of your life. You no longer Own your business, but its rather you are owned by someone.

It's a trap – you spend more to earn role – Result in borrowing more to fill the gap.

Ultimately your income goes in repayment of your debt & interest payment, thus you keep borrowing to maintain your cycle of productivity & lifestyle. Which ultimately gives you stress & lead to Disaster? This is called a spiral trap of interest.

It's a bad cycle – A Vicious cycle. Once you get into debt it's difficult to come out of this vicious trap. One very big corporate leader termed Interest/ Loan, as a cancerous cell of the business. We take maximum loans during Boom time & face Multi—Year losses during Recession.

DO WE REALLY NEED EXTERNAL FINANCIAL ASSISTANCE?

Since the subject is very vast and diverse I will limit myself to the two basic ingredients required to be successful in the present competitive business environment, and how to overcome the financial obstacles for MSME

1. Operational Management
2. Financial Management

Both of these issues are very core in nature, or in my opinion they are absolute heart and soul of a successful venture. Unfortunately, we have grave misconceptions about these basic management principles in our minds, and thereby have a very limited view of what exactly construes as to what is true way to grow our business in an ethical financial environment. This is because we have compartmentalized the whole concept of business into illusory blocks.

Operational Management is the process that generally plans, controls and supervise manufacturing and production processes and service delivery. It's important in a business process as it helps effectively in managing, control and supervise good services and people.

Financial Management is basically Financial prudence, whereby a proper planning in advance and investing in areas where you can expect high returns. It also means having complete knowledge about the money you have and how you can make it grow.

OPERATIONAL MANAGEMENT: -

* Steady Growth: - i.e. Good long-term growth rate
i.e. Steady Growth both during Boom time and recession time.
* Management Operational Approach
<u>Contrarian Approach</u> .... <u>Popular Approach</u>
- Operation – 60% .... Operations – 60%
- Productivity 20% ...... VS .... Productivity – 5%
- Growth – ... 20% .... Growth – 35%
* High ROCE – Steady growth .... Low ROCE – Excessive Growth
A% .... B% X% ....Y%
A>B X<Y
surplus in funds deficit in fund

Now let's understand with this most important aspects of dealing and Overcoming these obstacles.

Here the Keyword is Steady growth.

The mistake which we do is during good times we try to achieve unprecedented growth & then we de- growth during recession or bad times. A steady growth across the business cycle is good long-term growth of average 20% and How to achieve this is by our management approach of giving equal weightage to both productivity & growth. Generally, we falter on giving more weightage to growth rather than productivity which is the cause of De-growth during recession as we fail on productivity. Now taking above points into considerations if we increase our focus on productivity and Maintain Steady Growth our ROCE (Return On Capital Employed) will be high. So, our focus always should be to have ROCE > Growth and not the other way round. And the Business will always generate, Positive Cash flows and you avoid taking borrowed Money.

FINANCIAL MANAGEMENT: -
* Reducing Market Credit.
* Market Segmentation.
* Stock Management

finished good/WIP/Ready good.
* Production Management
- Identity the Issue
* Purchase Management
Reducing Market Credit is the basic tool of Financial Management

- The first Principal of Hzt Ab. Rahman Bin Auf (R.A) as a business Man was to deal only on Cash transaction. No Credit Buying or Credit Selling. We view goods transferred on credit to our Customers as Sales; in reality, it is just a stock transfer, as we have not been paid. Better option is to Rather Offer cash discount or Bulk discount & Push your Sales, and that to at Month End to fulfil targets. By offering credit sales, we also tend to lose sales as we stop supply to our customers for overdue payments. Other disadvantage is our sales force focus also gets diverted on collections.

- Concentrate on small Retailers for your strong cash flow by giving cash discounts & strong supply chain. Keep large Retailers on Credit but offer then volume discounts. In this way, your balance of payments will be maintained.

- As for Stock Management, again according to the Principal of Hzt Ab. Rehman Bin Auf (R.A), he never waited for higher profit or never Stock his goods. He always tried to avoid storage, because again Storage have its own cost, and by constant flow of sales It derives a high level of flow of Money. So, his Main Emphasis was on making earnings by increasing profits & thereby increasing Cash flow. High Finished Good (FG) & Work in Process (WIP) Stock Leads to high dead Stock & carrying Cost. Further high FG stock causes us to offer promotion / Schemes for Liquidating the stock thereby reducing our Margins.

- Our major flaw is we produce stock when sales are insufficient. As our production pattern is not in line with sales. Our high WIP stock results in long lead time. For production which affects our poor service levels.

- Purchasing Raw Material and negotiating with suppliers is the key to your healthy cash flow. Focus on Price, lead time, quantity, frequency of order are important tools for negotiation. Reduce Production lead time at your supplier's end. Build a long-term relationship with suppliers thereby improving reliability of supply.

If all these above factors are taken care of in most professional way I don't think we will need any borrowed capital for our growth plan.

ALTERNATE METHODS OF FUNDING:

After understanding the financial management system & disadvantages of borrowed funds, lets know the alternative methods of funding which can serve as a lifeline to small business. These alternative finance option can be equity based or non-equity based.

EQUITY BASED :

Initial Public Offering SME Exchange
Venture Capital: - (a) Well-Off Investor.
(b) Investment Banks.
(c) Financial Institution.
Angel Investors: - (a) Individual Leaders in Entrepreneurial system.
(b) CEO's of successful venture.
Crowd funding: - (a) Multiple Individuals through social media platform.
& P2P Lending (b) Small amounts raise from large pool of individual.
Hybrid Financing: - (a) It's a Combo of Equity + debt.
(b) Very well, can be structured in a sharia compliant form.

NON-EQUITY BASED:

Ijara (Leasing) 1) A Sharia Compliant Product for Leasing
2) Financial Lease & Operational Lease
3) Zero Down Payment
4) 100% Tax Deduction on Lease Rentals

Musharkah: - 1) A form of joint Venture.
2) Profit Sharing based Financing for Working Capital &
Projects
3) It's a concept of Sharing Risks and Rewards.

Asset Financing: - Its generally used to cover short term need for working capital

Invoice Factoring: - It's a way for Business to Borrow Money against the dues from Customers

SME Exchange: -

In 2010, it was recommended by PMO task force. It was established to provide opportunity to entrepreneurs to raise equity capital for growth & expansion of SME's. A very simple & doable listing guideline. Only post-issue face value capital of Rs.1 Crore to maximum 25 Cr. Net tangible arrests of 1 cr. Net worth at least 1 cr, with a track record of profit distribution to at least 2 years out of 3 years, if not then net worth should be 3 cr. So, with such basic guidelines it is a very good opportunity for SME's to raise equity on this platform.

Venture Capital: -
This is a private equity which is generally provided to start-up companies and small businesses that have long term growth potential. It cannot always be in monetary form but it can be in form of providing technical or managerial expertise. There is no Interest outflow but there could be an exit clause.

Angel Investors: -

These set of investors are basically leader in Entrepreneurialsystem having strong operational expertise of leading new & successful ventures. They are passionate individual to create scale & value for start-ups. They invest in a very early stage businesses which have potential to create a huge value.

Crowd Funding: -

A very recent concept & a practice of funding a project of ventures by raising small amounts of money from large numbers of people, typically through Internet or Social media platform. And more it is used to raise charity funds. According to rules in India equity based crowd funding is illegal. But we have a classic case of Momin Community of Gujarat practicing this sort of community funding on the principles of crowd funding, and it is very successful to date. But on similar lines we have P2P lending which is regulated by RBI. You need to study various sites for P2P lending. So, alternate to crowd funding is P2P. It's a practice of lending money to individuals or businesses through online services that match lenders with borrowers. Websites that facilitate P2P lending has greatly increased its adoption as an alternate method of financing.

Hybrid Finance: -

As the name suggest it's a combination of equity & debt. Various forms of hybrid finance like preference shares convertible debentures, Warrants and so on can also be structured in a sharia compliant way. One very good option being Sukuk, Asset Backed shariah compliant Bonds. These Non-Equity based products, helps you in maintaining your equity structure in a company. It helps in Unlocking your Capital and most important its compliant with all Indian laws and regulations.

Ijara: -

It's nothing but a modern concept of Leasing. There are 2 types of Lease- Financial Lease and Operational Lease. In financial Lease agreement, ownership of the asset is transferred to Lessee, But in Operational Lease the asset is retained by lessor at the end of the agreement. It's the most simple and easy mode of Sharia Financing.

Musharkah

Asset Financing & Invoice factoring: -

These both are rampantly used by businesses in today's world. Asset financing is for short term need of Working Capital, by leveraging investments, inventory and using it for working Capital. Similar Invoice Factoring is done to leverage the accounts receivables from customers for better mobilization of funds in re investing in operations or improving productivity by paying to Suppliers. These both form of products can be made Sharia compliant by way of Murabaha Finance. Murabaha also referred to as cost-plus financing. Both parties agree to the cost and mark-up of an Asset. As such it's not an Interest-bearing Loan but a very acceptable form of Credit Sale under Islamic Law. In Today's world Murabaha has become most popular financing technique with Islamic Banks.

CONCLUSION:

It's all about choosing the right Product that can Support your businesses where there is downturn to Revenue.
Furthermore, these alternate funding solutions offer:
diversification in terms of lenders, Maturity and Security Package
AND Lastly
Strengthen the financial Structure of your Business Enterprise.

Sustainability of Business and its long-term Growth Plans:

Everyone runs into obstacles, but the way you deal with them will determine whether you trip and fall, or overcome them unscathed.

What can we do to close the door on these obstacles so we can capitalize on our opportunities to succeed? Companies need to think and act across different Horizons

1. **Resolve**: Address the immediate challenges that represents to organisation's workforce, customers, technology and Business partners/stakeholders
2. **Resilience**: Address near term cash-management challenges and broader resiliency issues during recessionary periods; shutdowns or economic knock on effects
3. **Reimagination**: Reimagination has the Ability to Optimize an Organization While Removing Bottlenecks and Unnecessary Process Dependencies. Digital transformation puts technology at the core of business strategy. This approach can **reduce operating expenses and inefficiency**. It could even change the course of your business. With a unified model across business and technology, it's easier to achieve future ambitions.
4. **Reforms:** The broader aim is to boost investor confidence, foster employee friendly climate within an organisation and be clear about regulatory frame work, a strong Risk Management Process needs to be in place to have Business Continuity Plans and creating competitive environments of healthy competition through a system of assessing employees through well designed KPI's

Business and Financial Planning

- Organization has to have goals clearly defined as short term, medium term and long term
- Align your strategy based on the goals
- The goals need to be split into various sub section with well-defined objectives
- Each goal needs to be budgeted with a horizon of 1-5 years outlook
- Goals to include

- Revenue Growth
- Expense management
- Expansion plans
- Competition Landscape
- Joint Ventures, Collaboration, M&A
- Deployment of Funds

- Employee Management (Retention, Training,)

- Periodic forecast to revise the budget based on the current business scenario normally for a year
- Reviews required periodically to track Actuals vs Budgets & forecast

CASH MANAGEMENT

Without generating adequate cash to meet its needs, a business will find it difficult to conduct routine activities such as paying suppliers, buying raw materials, and paying its employees, let alone making investments. And it should have sufficient cash to pay dividends and keep its investors happy. Cash Conservation is critical for the success of a business enterprise. The objectives of cash management are straightforward – maximise liquidity and control cash flows and maximise the value of funds while minimising the cost of funds. The strategies for meeting such objectives include varying degrees of long-term planning requirements.

Cash Conservation for small business and maintain healthy cash flow management

- Pay bills strategically. …
- Choose the right payroll cycle. …
- Negotiate your payments with suppliers and even creditors
- Collect receivables quickly and improve collection process
- Manage your credit policies carefully to avoid interest exposures if any
- Review your insurances for business interruptions
- Protect forex exposure through hedge
- Use technology to make and accept payments.

Cash flow is more forward-looking, showing how much cash your business generates over a specific period. working capital gives you a snapshot of your company's current financial health — insight about how quickly your company can withstand unforeseen market disruptions.

Working capital is the difference between the company's current assets— including cash and other assets that can be converted into cash within a year — and its current liabilities, working capital affects many aspects of your business, from paying your employees and vendors to keeping the lights on and planning for sustainable long-term growth. In short, working capital is the money available to meet your current, short-term obligations. Positive working capital generally indicates that organization is able to fulfil its short-term liabilities.

BUSINESS EXPANSION

Growth can allow a business to expand into new geographic markets, acquire more customers, or provide the next level of service to existing customers that they've been asking for. Growing your brand brings value to the business and quality to customers. Workers often want to be part of a growing, successful company. Overall, the benefits of expanding a business include **reducing external risks** (such as those posed by competition, the market, or technology changes). Expansion can also enhance the impression of greater financial viability: larger businesses often look more appealing to investors and lenders.

Business Expansion can be a plain vanilla growth or Backward/Forward Integration. It can be either through fresh equity infusion or internal accruals. Economies of scale are achieved in view of Business expansion which can be leveraged. Any incentives/ packages offered by government should be availed.

All Future expansions has to be coupled with proper market research and meticulous planning. A proper Analysis is of utmost importance before executing a business expansion plans. If needed consider taking views of experts and market players and also whether expansion plans should be executed or to wait for an opportune time.

Customer and their preferences need to be understand first, also explore value addition to the products/services such as accreditation, alliances, or new inputs in products.

TEAM MANAGEMENT

Employees are Valuable Assets of an Organization and the Key to Success. They are the ones who contribute effectively towards the successful functioning of an organization. They strive hard to deliver their level best and achieve the assigned targets within the stipulated time frame. This means their strength, commitment and dedication, and their emotional connection with the organization can't be judged as assets in monetary value.

Effective communication can increase employee engagement, boost workplace productivity, and drive business growth. Communication is the cornerstone of an engaged workforce. A company's workforce represents its most significant investment and ultimately determines the success or failure of the organization.

- Align the Team with organisational goals
- A proper and regular interaction between Team and its reporting Manager to identify improvement areas and their training needs
- Motivate employees of having right and positive attitude
- Encourage cross functional working
- Organise events for creating strong bonding between employees and various teams
- Share business updates with employees periodically
- Have a regular open house meet
- Constant communication has to be kept with employees

ADAPTABILITY OF TECHNOLOGY

Technology helps increase the efficiency of systems, products and services. It helps track and streamline processes, maintain data flow and manage contacts and employee records. In fact, this increased efficiency in operation helps reduce costs as well as enable the business to grow rapidly. Technology solutions allow small businesses to remain agile and quick to respond to change within the markets. Integration of various tech leads to increased collaboration among teams leading to better product development.

It's important to adapt to technology and move with the changing time, as flexibility is the key to success in today's time.

Future belongs to Artificial Intelligence (AI), Cloud, Robotic Process Automation, and Internet. They are now part of our life and expected to invade more rapidly.

Social Media, Mobile, Analytics and Cloud technologies will have more prominence. Businesses will move from brick and mortar to Virtual World, with Cyber security to be layer above information Technology.

It's time we retain Expertise and Learn New AREAS, and be keen to take new areas outside finance. Be updated for any regulatory, technological or business changes by attending seminars, webinars, surfing internet, networking through business associations and chambers, and lot of Reading content.

RISK MANAGEMENT

Businesses face many risks; therefore, risk management should be a central part of any business' strategic management. Risk management helps you to identify and address the risks facing your business and in doing so increase the likelihood of successfully achieving your businesses objectives and also ensuring Business Continuity.

Business continuity refers to strategic planning, which is structured to ensure business as usual when any disaster occurs. Hence a strong Risk Management process needs to be in place to have Business continuity plans.

Risks can be graded into Low, Medium, Critical.

Here are five types of business risk that every company should address as part of their strategy and planning process.

- Security and fraud risk.
- Compliance risk.

- Operational risk.
- Financial or economic risk.
- Reputational risk.

WEALTH MANAGEMENT

A proper wealth management can help you develop a financial plan that includes saving, investing and spending goals. It can also help you plan for retirement, saving for other major life events. These plans can be revisited periodically as your circumstances change. And a proper Tax advice. Wealth management helps in reducing financial stress and prioritize financial decisions based on a timeframe. **Retirement planning** is central to wealth management and individuals must start saving early, taking risks in investments while young and getting more conservative when retirement age approaches.

Prudent ways to save and increase your hard-earned money, so that your wealth provides a safety net in dire times:

Plan, Plan, and Plan

While endless and mindless splurging on your favourite things is extremely tempting, it is just as dangerous and reckless. Your expensive hobbies or your ever-growing shopping won't rescue you in times of financial stress.

Hence, start out with an assessment of your income, liabilities, and risks and chalk out a plan that details your financial goals, the amount required to achieve them and the duration. This will enable you to take control of your income and expenses and have an effective investment strategy to ensure a comfortable retirement and achieve other goals.

A sudden financial windfall makes us want to spend more since we feel it will last forever. But, having your life mapped out financially ensures that you can foresee what's coming and stay away from habits that put your financial health in danger. Making money is much easier than preserving and saving it for the long term. It takes ages to earn wealth, but only seconds to squander it. As Robert Kiyosaki puts it, "It's not how much money you make, but how much money you keep, how hard it works for you, and how many generations you keep it for."

Invest Hard

Do not discount the power of patience, time, and compounding. Investing allows you to harness the power of compounding, which is simply earning profit on your profit, and significantly multiplying your gains in the long run. In fact, Warren Buffett, perhaps the richest investor on this planet, credits his extensive wealth to compounding.

Investing allows you to harness the power of compounding. Let's say you invest just Rs 5,000 per month (SIP) Systematic Investment Plan in the market for 20 years. At 12 percent assumed returns, you'll end up earning more than Rs 37,00,000 over your invested total of Rs 12,00,000, taking your overall gains to nearly Rs 50,00,000!

Most of us like to increase our expenses when we get a raise. Instead, increase your investments every time you earn more, and **Become financially responsible**

IX

LEADERSHIP – AND ITS ATTRIBUTES

The true attributes of a good leader are very well described in Quran.

- ...Show integrity for the sake of Allah, bearing witness with Justice. Do not let hatred for a people incite you into becoming unjust. *Quran 5:8*
- ...If you judge, judge between them justly. Allah loves the Just. *Quran 5:42*

Good Leaders are good and honest followers, humble, Piety, truthful, simple and they realise that success only comes from God the almighty, it's their faith.

There is a system of leadership based on the principal of trust. Effective leadership is about executing company's vision and setting the tone and the culture for that particular organisation. Leadership means creating and planning, securing resources and looking out for and improving errors.

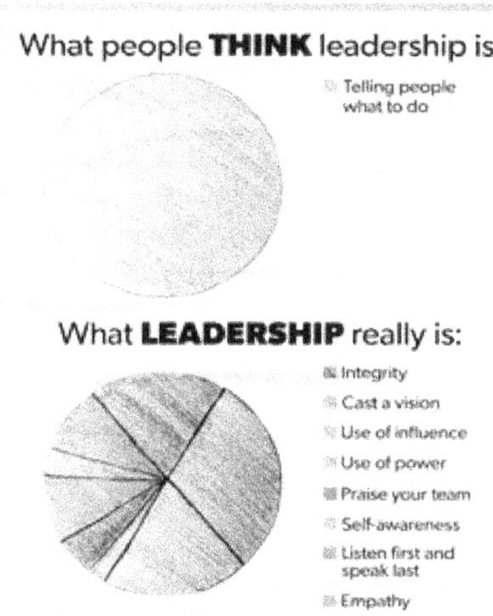

LEADERSHIP TRAITS:

The strength of an Ethical mind set is that it has within itself as a reason for existence a sophisticated methodology for restraining the Ego, something that Capitalism and Socialism never had.

Unfortunately, we have grave misconceptions about what a ethical mind-set is, and thereby have a very limited view of what exactly construes, as to what an Ethical mind-set can be. This is because we have compartmentalised the whole concept of Ethics, honesty and integrity into illusory Blocks.

- Faith: Faith in God and faith in its people
- Character and Conduct between 2 humans
- Creating conducive Environment, Building of society/ Organisation, equality and justice for all
- Clear in Dealings, more particularly business ethics and financial dealings

The person with these strong humanitarian attributes is an ideal for a leadership Role.

How Leaders win people

1. Sell vision/Cause in terms of 'real benefit to an organisation'
2. Let others take credit for ideas (Ahsan)
3. Use suggestions rather than orders (Consultation)
4. Avoid arguments (Controls anger)
5. Help people solve their problems ongoing coaching (Knowledge, Wisdom and Skill)

Thus, from these 5 points we can evolve the Rules of a true Leader
RULES OF LEADERSHIP:
Set examples of the leadership:

- Know yourself and seek self-improvement.

- Make sound and timely decision.

- Set the examples.

- know your people and look out for their well being.

- Keep your workers informed.

- Develop sense of responsibility in workers.

- Ensure task are understood and done.

- Train as a team.

- Use fall capability of organization.

- Be technically proficient.

- Seek responsibility and take responsibility of your action.

When you are responsible for a team of People, it is important to be straightforward. Your company and its employee are a reflection of yourself, and if you make honest and ethical behaviour as a key value your team will follow.

A just and Ethical leader don't charge forward without others, he mobilizes others and continually inspire them to strive toward the destination. Good leaders don't wait around for others to guide them. They take the initiative and demonstrate the courage and fortitude to make things happen.

Leadership Qualities:

Empathy: Truly great leaders have enough open- mindedness to understand their follower's motivations, hopes, dreams and problems

Confidence: When Leaders exhibit confidence, they typically feel positive about their ability to lead people and deal with daily challenges. They have a "can do" attitude about whatever comes their way. Their tem members appreciate working with an upbeat and upright leader who holds a positive vision.

Integrity: Leaders with integrity act in accordance with their words, they practice what they preach, and own up to their mistakes, as opposed to hiding them, blaming their team or making excuses, and they garner trust among their colleagues.

Accountability: When you make people accountable for their actions you're effectively teaching them to value their work. When done right accountability can increase your team members skills and confidence. High levels of accountability especially among leaders builds trust and instils high level of confidence in team members and ultimately within organisation.

Other than these qualities there are certain Rules for an Aspiring Leader and 1st Generation Entrepreneur

1. Define and always stay true to your values. These values will determine the legacy of your entrepreneurial journey.
2. Never fear to think big. An aspiring leader has to do lot of catching up. And can never think of avoiding risk
3. Set higher goals as it helps attract like-minded people, don't get bogged down thinking about risk
4. Invest in relationship
5. Spend time effectively in nurturing your business, and people
6. Commit to higher cause so your teams and you can eventually feel you contributed to something more than a business
7. Take full responsibility of your actions, as you will create your own destiny

BE A MODERN AND A NEW AGE LEADER:

OLD SCHOOL OF THOUGHTS	NEW AND DYNAMIC APPROACH
Employees are biggest threat	Employees biggest Assets
Top down communication	Open Communication
Skill over Behaviour	Behaviour over skills
Manage Time	Empower Results
Rigid working schedule	Flexible working schedule
At your Desk	Mobility
Work for weekend	Do something you love
Corporate Jargon	Genuine Honesty
Double Standard	One Standard
Fear of Failure	Take failure head on
Enrich Shareholders/	Enrich lives

The Life Purpose of a True Leader:
A true leader has 4 main purpose of Professional life:

- Profession
- Passion
- Mission
- Vocation

For his Profession and Vocation, he is paid for it
But he loves to fulfil his Mission through his Passion
Hence, he is Great at his Profession as it is his Passion
Thus, the World needs his vocation which is his mission
This Life purpose creates 12 outstanding Habits of a Productive and Efficient Leader

- They Review What Worked
- They Recognise what don't work
- They meticulously Plan

- They Anticipate obstacles and come up with a solution
- They write things down
- They Prioritize work
- They do one thing at a time
- They set boundaries
- They automate and delegate
- They don't hesitate to ask questions
- They develop Keystone habits
- They commit to continuous improvement

These outstanding habits creates a creative mind of an efficient Leader. What causes Creativity

1. Confidence: Ability to question without fear
2. Observation: Seeing Problems/Ideas
3. Humility: Knowing you don't know everything
4. Mindfulness: Thinking on how to think
5. Curiosity: Exploring and Experimenting
6. Resourcefulness: Something to tinker with
7. Energy: Never say Die attitude
8. Action: Not just thinking but Doing Implementing ideas

Be a Complete Leader

A complete Leader is one who is in control of Overall Leadership. Which consists of:

- **Organizational leadership**: An organisational leader leads in managing overall Performance and evaluating staff performance whereby Developing Talent and Drives for Result

- **Strategic Leadership**: It inspires Strategic thinking and planning, and inspiring and sharing his vision, which leads to fruitful decision making

- **Managing Self/Others**: Full of Empathy towards his team, always open to Change and leads his personal drive to inspire his sub ordinates

- **Knowledge Base Leadership**: Provider of Overall and Technical Knowledge, thereby gives direction to its business perspective and also to

Environment and Industry specific perspective

- **Practice Evaluation:** Formally leads the way in Client Development, Market development, which strengthens business Development, and improves the sales Development programmes

A successful and efficient Leader will take Failures in his own stride and overcome it in a very Sporting way

- He accepts that Failures and Setbacks will occur and one need to overcome them
- He very well recognises that success and Failures are on the same path
- Give your efforts in working towards your Goals. Focus lee on its outcome
- He very well understands that setback or failure does not define me as a person

Let's look at some short inspiring stories about leadership that can help us to be a good, better, best leaders. Though we might have read, heard or seen these stories on internet but sometimes we don't give importance to such stories.

A. In Leadership, we have heard lot above Faith, Trust, Hope, Confidence, Attitude etc. But how can we actually define them?

Let's see these 6 LITTLE STORIES actually one liners story for our easy understanding

{1} ONCE, all villagers decided to pray for rain, on the day of prayer all the People gathered but only one boy came with an umbrella.

That's

FAITH

{2} WHEN You throw a baby in the air, she laughs because she knows you will catch her.

That's

TRUST

3} EVERY Night we go to bed, without any assurance of being alive the next Morning but still we set the alarms to wake up.

That's

HOPE

{4} WE Plan big things for tomorrow in spite of zero knowledge of the future.

That's

CONFIDENCE

{5} WE See the world suffering. But still we get Married.

That's

LOVE

{6} On an Old Man's shirt was written a cute sentence 'I Am Not 60 Years Old., I Am Sweet 16 with 44 years' Experience.'

That's

ATTITUDE

(B) We have read number of times how an effective leader stimulates his team. A successful team is created by establishing Teamwork, Humanity, Empathy and Equality. The interpersonal behavior of the team members is a key to a successful organization.

This story again was taken from some internet source which I THOUGHT will gives us a great insight and inspiration to be a part of a successful and effective Team

8 boys were standing on a race track for racing.

Ready! Steady! Bang!

With sound of Pistol all boys started running.

Hardly had they covered 10 to 15 steps, 1 boy slipped & fell, and He started crying due to pain.

When other 7 Boys heard him, all of them STOPPED running...

STOOD for a while, turned BACK & RAN towards him.

All the 7 Boys LIFTED the Boy,

pacified him, joined hands together, walked together & reached WINNING Post.

Officials were shocked. Many Eyes were filled with tears.

It happened at Pune. Race was conducted by National Institute of Mental Health...

All participants were DIFFERENTLY- ABLED.

What did they teach?

• Teamwork,

- Humanity,
- Sportsman spirit,
- Love,
- Care,
- &
- Equality...

Can We do this? We Surely can NEVER Do this,
because...
We are Mentally....affected with Ego... and Attitude
Be a true Leader and lead a team just like these 8 Differently abled Boys, empty out all the Goodness that is within you. Deliver it to the world as I always say Sharing is caring.
If You Have an Idea perform it
If you have knowledge share it
If you have a Goal, achieve it
Love, Share, and Distribute, do not keep it inside you
Shall we begin to give and remove and spread every atom of Goodness within us?
Start the journey of a true Business Leader with an exceptional entrepreneurial quality.

X

EMPOWERING WOMEN WITH BUSINESS ENTREPRENEURSHIP

Are we wondering how to empower women so that they can move towards a better future?

And this is also a fact that, Women are deprived of some very basic workplace rights,<u>reveals a pan-India study</u> of over 43,000 females across sectors and socioeconomic strata. Sample this: 48% of women healthcare workers and one in three policewomen don't have toilet facilities. Similarly, a significant percentage of working women don't have canteen, transportation, or security provisions. More than one in 10 women face <u>sexual harassment</u> at the workplace. Crime against women are on the rise, but lac of urgency to curtail this heinous crime is a road block, despite this there's a huge movement among women itself to empower one another, to secure equal rights, to challenge gender narratives and to establish a brighter future. Work Hard, do your tasks alone, gain Knowledge about more and more fields, walk alone with confidence and push your limits. "Don't beg for equality, establish it". It's clear we need to make changes and It's time to empower women in our community and around the world.

- Boost their self esteem
- Shut down the negativity

- Be open and honest
- Advocate for female colleagues
- Help and provide basic necessities to women workforce
- Support women run business enterprises

Empowering women is important for the health and social development of families, and communities. When women are safe fulfilled and living a productive life, they reach their full potential. Empowering Girls is key to economic growth, political stability and social transformation.

Women are the Largest untapped reservoir of talent in the world....
Hilary Clinton

Women Entrepreneur is any woman who organizes and Manages any enterprise, especially business.... Research shows that woman owned companies generate higher revenues than those owned by men. Experts at Boston Consulting Group also found that women are more effective as a leader and are better at creating jobs.

According to Caliper study of the qualities that distinguish women leaders, it shows women leaders as more assertive and persuasive, have a stronger need to get things done and are more willing to take risk than their male counterparts. They are better in facilitating collaboration and information sharing.

An Ethical women entrepreneur always adhered to ethical work-related values of Good and hard work, honesty and truthfulness, fairness and justice, and benevolence.

According to Islamic studies too it can be said that Islam is not against women working or engaging themselves or contributing their worth in business related activities. In fact, as I had mentioned in my Introductory Chapter, the first wife of the Prophet Mohammed (SAW) Khadija was very successful business woman in her own right, who controlled one of the most important caravan trade routes in the region. She is the shining example of a strong independent muslin woman with an entrepreneurial spirit

It's the need of the hour to encourage women to participate in entrepreneurial activities for economic prosperity and social growth. Though their participation in economic activities is very less than men globally, as entrepreneurial field was regarded as male dominant sector. Entrepreneurship flourishes due to economic, social, and environmental factors while the practice of ethical principles works as a catalyst in this process. Women entrepreneurship helps in alleviating poverty and unemployment that leads to socio-economic prosperity in a country.

Women engagement in different business activities can not only empower them socially and financially but can also share the household economic burden with men. Further it also helps them to make their decisions independently. They can also use the option of partnering within the family for the financial and social network. The challenges faced by these women entrepreneurs can be handled with their family support.

Most important attributes of a Business women

SELF BELIEF:

Any successful businesswomen you see, will discover how much they believe in themselves. If you don't believe that you can succeed, then you won't go far enough.

Mary Kay Ash founder of Mary Kay Cosmetics build her business just a month after her husband's death. She says if you think you can? then you can. And if you think you can't, then fine its end of your story. Self-belief is probably the single most important quality possessed by any successful entrepreneur. To be successful female entrepreneur you have to believe in yourself and believe that whatever you are doing is making a difference. There is no point starting a business unless you possess a strong sense of belief and purpose. You have to believe that you are destined for great things and good for the community.

AMBITION:

Always strive to push forward. Always aim for the top.... What's stopping you? Never settle for second best. Have courage to be as ambitious as Men.

Boldness is more beautiful than beauty. So be strong , be Bold, and Be Ambitious.

CONFIDENCE:

Your confidence will win people's respect, earn their trust and gain you a solid reputation.

Your Body language while walking into a room, greeting people and your eye contact should be brimming with confidence.

Confidence is most essential ingredient to win clients and build a profitable business.

PASSION:

Successful business women are always passionate about what they do as they create businesses around things they enjoy. Find your own passion, believe in it and turn it into something you can really be proud of.

To succeed you have to believe in something with such a passion that it becomes a reality.

HUMILITY:

Successful businesswomen will always be humble. They are never afraid to admit they don't know everything and will always be eager to learn and strive to boost their skills.

HARD WORK:

Remember "Hard work beats Talent"
When
"Talent doesn't work Hard"

You can have exceptional intelligence, or great connections, you have great opportunities, but in the end, hard work is the true enduring characteristics of a successful person. Hard Work is the secret to success.

Be prepared for long hours and sacrificing your spare time to build up a business

COURAGEOUS:

It really takes gut to run a business, means you have to take risk and accept that when things go wrong you can always survive and turnaround. Be Brave and you will never look back. You need to constantly push yourself out of your comfort zone to move forward.

SUSTAINABILITY:

To start a venture is one thing and to keep going and sustain is another matter entirely. You need to be persistence with NEVER GIVE UP ATITTUDE. When your chips are down, remind yourself of all your past achievements

CASE STUDIES OF WOMEN ENTREPRENEUR

Women have started doing all kinds of businesses such as **accounting, wedding planning, fitness trainer** and what not. The options are endless but what you find interesting, is the most important factor. Any woman can commence with any business; all she needs is knowledge and research about the work that you start.

Some Good Business Ideas for Women

- Tiffin Services/Food Business.
- Pet Grooming/Training.
- Yoga Instructor.
- Clothes Business.
- Beauty Parlour.
- Organic Cosmetics/Toiletries.
- Consultancy/Counselling Business.
- Data Entry Business.

Launch of Association of Women Entrepreneur is formed to support and connect Muslim Women entrepreneurs; To empower Dawoodi Bohra women a platform, where women would be able to do business has been created. There are many women entrepreneurs in Bohra community who take advantage of such platforms. There were quite a few women selling online, there was no single platform for wider reach. These such platforms also help women in city, as they can now sell their products from the comfort of their own homes.

Young women, Aasha, with an M.Sc. DEGREE WORKING AS AN ADMINISTRATOR IN A HOSPITAL TILL 2017, away from family in a far-off location and craving for home food every single day, has turned the stereotypical role of a women in the kitchen, into a successful business that delivers homemade food to corporate offices. It's on the lines of Mumbai's famous dabbawallahs, but uses the platform of Porter and Dunzo to deliver it. They develop a unique selling point in their service which promise of the menu not being repeated for an entire month.

One women's story I came across, where she convinced her family not to waste money on funds kept for her wedding but rather to invest in her business Start-up Manufacturing Cloth Sanitary Pads and providing employment to 25 to 30 women from economically weaker section, thereby providing them with an opportunity to earn a good livelihood.

Baking is one such activity, which has shown the way to passionate Girls and women to venture out, had convert their hobbies and passion into a business opportunity. Their message is loud and clear..." If we can do this, why not you all can... As women, they feel we need to be seen and heard, to become an entrepreneur and become financially independent. Also, FASHION DESIGNING If yes, start your fashion business and get paid handsomely by helping your clients turn into fashionistas. Fashion designing is one of the most money-making small business ideas for women that requires very little investment.

When a young house-wife decided to become an entrepreneur some 20 years ago she began by sourcing cotton dress materials and other fabrics from the local wholesale suppliers within the city that would appeal in terms of design, patterns and most important pricing to her closed acquaintances, friends, and neighbours. Her unique selling point was her Return Policy if it was not liked by the customer. Her mode of sales operation was, low margin and fast turnover, and no credit policy. She bought her stock on consignment basis only. i.e. Payment to suppliers once goods sold and return the unsold stuff. This way she created a strong cash flow management system. Her advertisement was purely by word of mouth due to her honesty, straight forward attitude and humbleness. Now after 2 decades of humble beginning this house-wife fulfilling her regular duties and raising 2, now adult daughters has established her name not only in her city but to far of places like Bengaluru, Kolhapur, Vadodara, Mumbai with a wide range of products like fabrics, unstitched dresses, Bedsheets, Towels, Blankets, and lot more. Now thanks to the emergence of digital platforms like Instagram, WhatsApp she has been getting more orders after putting up her products on Instagram page of hers by name "Patterns and Crafts" She has developed her own WhatsApp Group and WhatsApp community for broadcasting her new range products once in a week.

A Young Graduate in her late twenties, with majors in Accounting, started Macramé form of art couple of years back as a hobby which gradually turned into passion and then business.

She is owning a Macramé Business under the brand name Knot-it-All @Qudsazz, a registered Trademark. At Knot-it-All, she makes elegant home decor product using macramé technique that uses knots to create various textiles. It is an art of knotting to create beautiful art pieces to give a contemporary look. All the pieces she makes are of high quality. She also offers customization to suit customer requirement. Her few products are listed on Amazon, and also on Instagram.

My process of making art is by sheer feedback of my customers' requirements. Generating new ideas takes time and effort, so I need to know my customers mind and how they value the creativity. How they recognise and value my creativity, so basically, it's a collaboration between me and my customers...Says Qudsiya

Further she elaborates that, every home is Beautiful, and so there should be beautiful art pieces around. At Knot_it_All, you can look around for beautifully crafted macramé art work which will make your home and garden come alive with colours. She makes a variety of products to suit your needs perfectly and if she doesn't have it, she will make it as per your request.

According to her: Art is important as it gives you beauty of freedom. It is free expression of human mind and senses. It gives me creative thinking and this creative art motivates me primarily by interest, self-satisfaction and challenge of the work itself, and not by the external pressures, Money can be a strong motivator especially when years of work go into mastering your art, and people are willing to pay for your talents, it helps to get motivated to be more creative.

As I come from Ahmedabad which is a historical city approx. 611 years old and India's first and only world heritage city. This heritage tag of my city inspires to do something unique archaic and contemporary feel of my work. And Macramé is a crafting technique that uses knots to create various textiles. Materials used include chords made of cotton twine, linen, jute, or yarn, which again is the uniqueness of my city as it is a textile hub, and was always known as Manchester of East.

APPENDIX

APPENDIX

A} Chart of Authority:

It is basically a segregation of Duties. The company shall delegate to discharge the duties in accordance to the laid down principles and approved by Board of Directors or the competent authority in accordance with Chart of Authority and responsibilities assigned to the departments.

Chart of Authority Approved on			

1.	Management		Authority	Limits (RO)
1.1	Business Strategy / Investment Policies / Asset Allocation Plans	Approval Review & Monitoring	BOD CEO	
1.2	Business Plan & Operational Budgets	Approval Review & Monitoring Reporting	BOD CEO	
1.3	Company Auditors	Appointment	BOD/CEO	
1.4	Company Legal Advisors	Appointment Initiate proceeding to protect company interest	BOD CEO	

2	Financial		Authority	Limits (RO)
2.1	Bank Accounts	Bank accounts opening with new banks	BOD	
		Bank account opening and closing with existing banks	CEO	
2.2	Authorised Cheque signatures	Approve category basis:	BOD Chairman - BOD BOD CEO VP-F&A Other VPs Manager-Ops	
2.2.A	New borrowing from banks	Secured against company assets	BOD CEO	
2.2 B	Capital Expenditure	Within approved budget	BOD	
			CEO with VP-F&A	
		Unapproved	BOD	
			CEO with VP-F&A Max per annum	
2.3	Accounts receivables / bad debts write off		BOD EC CEO with VP-F&A	

				Limits (RO)
2.4	Operating expenditure	Within approved budget (overall excluding provisions)	CEO with VP-F&A	
		Unapproved budget (overall per month)	BOD	
			CEO with VP-F&A	
			CEO with VP-F&A	
2.5	Payroll related matters	Within approval	CEO with VP-F&A	
2.6	Settlement of disputes	Approval	BOD	
			CEO with VP-F&A	

4	Aftersales / Manufacturing		Authority	Limits (RO)
4.1	Maintaining the Organizational chart, position of each employee and Job description	Approval GM's or Service Manager	CEO with VP-Admin or HR Head	
4.2	Workshop Organization (Booking, Tool Room, Workshop Equipments, etc.)	Workshop Controller	General Manager/ Service Manager	
4.3	Maintaining Control Board	Workshop Controller	General Manager/ Service Manager	
4.8	Parts & other Purchase & Sales	Parts Manager	Gen. Manager / C.E.O	
4.9	Parts Organization & Processes	Parts Manager	Gen. Manager	
4.10	Accounts and Cash	Accounts Dept.	C.E.O.	
4.11	Invoicing / Billing	Parts Manager & Service Advisor	Gen. Manager	
4.12	Credit Facilities to Individual & Corporate Customers	Service Manager	G.M. Aftersales / Finance Manager/ Admin.	
4.13	IT Activities and updates	IT In-charge	G.M. Aftersales / Admin.	
4.14	Stock yard organization and processes	Team Leaders / Service Advisor	Workshop Manager / Service Manager / GM. Aftersales.	

Chart of Authority Approved on				
6	**Administration**		**Authority**	**Limits (RO)**
6.1	Staff appointments & Terminations	CEO GM's and Above Staff	BOD CEO with HR Head	
6.2				
6.3				
6.4	Remuneration/Pay and benefits	CEO GM's & Above Staff	BOD CEO	
6.5	Performance appraisals	CEO GM's and Managers	BOD CEO	
6.6	Annual Leave	CEO GM's and Managers & Staff	Administration CEO	
6.7	Contract signing (Financial) Letters signing (non-financial)	Inquiry	CEO with VP-F&A Respective Level	

Legend:

BOD	- Board of Directors		VP-R	- Vice President
EC	- Executive Committee		M-OPS	- Mgr. Operations
CEO	- Chief Executive Officer			
VP-F&A	- Vice President Fin & Admin			

Note:
All EC approved authorities shall be exercised by the chairman EC or an EC member designated by him.
All delegated financial authority limits of the CEO shall be within the limits of the annual budget approved by BOD.
In the absence of the CEO, his authority will be delegated to senior most VP..
In general for approvals the policy of 'next level' up will be employed.

B] FINANCIAL CONTROL & PROCEDURE

- Description and assessment of the key financial systems and internal controls, including financial information supplied to management, estimating and forecasting procedures, cash management and the debtors and creditors control systems

- Cash Controls and Treasury Management

- Summaries of budgets, and compared with actual result for each year, together with comments on the main reasons for deviations from budgets

II PUBLISHED ACCOUNTS

The company account comprises of various reports, accounts, statements and notes required either by company law or accountancy profession

.

The format and contents of the balance sheet and profit & loss account are set by the companies' act 1985.

Parsoli would adopt all accounting policies and accounting methods laid down by the accounting profession through statements of Standards Accounting Practice (SSAP's) and Financial Reporting Standards (FRS's)

CASH FLOW STATEMENTS

Financial Reporting Standards No 1 (FRS 1) requires companies to include a cash flow statements. The standard calls for cash flow statements to split cash flows into the following headings

- Net cash flow from operating activities
- Return on investments and servicing of finance-(covering investment income, interest and dividends)
- Taxation
- Capital expenditure
- Management of liquid resources

ACCOUNTING RATIOS

Whilst the accounts by themselves give us useful information about a company, we at Parsoli proposes to find out more about the company by analysing key accounting ratios

III ACCOUNTING POLICIES:

A strong and transparent accounting Policies need to be in Place. It's a procedure implemented by a company's management team that are used to prepare its financial statements. These include any accounting methods, measurement systems, and procedures for presenting disclosures

1. **Accounting Convention**

The financial statements are prepared under the historical cost convention, on the accrual basis and materially complies with the mandatory accounting standards issued by Financial Reporting Standard No1 (FRS 1).

The preparation of the financial statements requires the management of the company makes estimates and assumptions that affect the reported amounts of income and expenses of the period and reported balances of assets and liabilities as the date of the financial statements. Management believes that the estimates used in the preparation of the financial statements are prudent and reasonable. Actual results could differ from these estimates.

1. **Inflation**

Assets and liabilities are recorder at historical cost to the Company. These costs are not adjusted to reflect the changing value in the purchasing power of money.

3. **Revenue Recognition**

    a. **Fee income arising from various services are recognised upfront on their becoming due.**
    b. **Income from Investments in instruments like Mutual Funds with assured returns, the income is accounted on an accrual basis.**
    c. **Dividend Income is accounted on accrual basis when the Company's right to receive the dividend is established.**
    d. **Interest Income is recognised as it accrues.**

4. **Investments**

Investments are capitalised at cost inclusive of brokerage and stamp charges and are classified in two categories, Current or Long Term. Current assets investments are at the lower of cost and net realisable value

Provision for diminution in the value of Investments is made in accordance to the issued guidelines

5. **Research and Development**

Research expenditure is written off to the profit and loss account in the year in which it is incurred. Development expenditure is written off in the same year unless the directors are satisfied as to the technical, commercial and financial viability of individual project. In this situation, the expenditure is deferred and amortised over the period from which the company is expected to benefit or the estimated useful life of the related asset.

6. Fixed Assets & Depreciation

Expenditure which are of capital in nature capitalised at cost.

Assets obtained under hire purchase contracts and finance leases are capitalised as tangible assets and depreciated over the shorter of the lease term and their useful lives. Obligations under such agreements are included in creditors net of the finance charge allocated to future periods. The finance element of the rental payment is charged to the profit and loss account so as to produce constant periodic rates of charge on the net obligations outstanding in each period.

For other assets depreciation is provided at rates calculated to write off the cost less residual value of each asset over its expected useful life as follows

Furniture, Fixtures & Equipments 15% reducing Balance

Motor Vehicles 25% reducing Balance

Computers 33% reducing Balance

Others (incl. Software & System Dev. Expenses) 25% reducing Balance

7. **Deferred Taxation**

Provision is made for deferred taxation using the liability method to take account of timing differences between the incidence of income and expenditure for taxation and accounting purpose except to the extent that the directors consider that a liability to taxation is unlikely to materialise.

IV Investment Policy

a. Evaluation of an investment proposal

The company to follow cautious and prudent policy in its investment/ deployment of funds decision. The investment will be considered and deliberated by a committee and decisions will be taken keeping in mind exposure to the single entity, industry and other relevant factors

b. Credit Policy

The Company's credit policy comprises of stringent criteria in appraising credit risk and fixing conservative norms for the company's credit exposure. The criteria for apprising credit risk are as follows

- Overall and individual exposure to each activity and client
- Security of the transactions

c. Provisioning Policy

- In respect of long term investment, reduction due to permanent decline is determined and provided for and is base on each investment individually
- Provisions is made for sub-standard doubtful and loss account in terms of the time and percentage factors and the amounts are provided for /written off accordingly

V Assumptions for Profitability Statements:
There are four basic assumptions of financial accounting.

- Economic activity
- Fiscal Period
- Going Concern
- Economic environment/RBI Monetary policy

Other than these above assumptions, some of the key expenses below are equally important because they form the building block on which financial accounting measurement is based

- Senior Management Costs and Recruitment Costs in Staff & Management Costs are assumed to increase 10% annually.
- Marketing & Business Development Cost, Finance & Administration Cost & Training & Development Cost is assumed to be increase by 5% per annum.
- Press Advertising Cost is assumed to increase by 3% every year.
- Similary Radio Advertising, TV Advertising & Outdoor Advertising is also assumed to increase by 3% per annum.
- Public Education / Relations Cost is also assumed to increase by 3% each year.

VI Key Factors

- **The company's one of the major activity to be identified and on the basis of its activity identify its exposure to credit and investment risks**
- **In the absence of any financial participation of the financial Institution/Bank, the monitoring of deployment of funds should be entirely to the Board of the Company**
- **The profitability of the company engaged in providing financial services is influenced by the general and monetary polices**
- **Competition from the existing and new player will have an impact on the business of the company**

APPENDIX

C} MODEL CODE OF CONDUCT

For all the Employees and Sr. Officers of the Company

I	This code of Conduct (hereinafter referred to as the "Code for the Employees and Sr. Officers of the Company) is laid down by the Board of Directors . The Code is aimed to set out the broad guidelines for the ethical business conduct by the Employees and Senior Officials of the Company and ensure compliance with the requirements specifically under the revised management policy with an underlying objective to discourage wrong practice and promote ethical conduct of the business of the Company. The Code is formulated in line with the interest of all the stakeholders of the Company namely, the shareholders, business partners and employees of the Company. The Code is applicable to the following persons, referred to as "Officers". 1. All the employees on the payroll of the Company; 2. All Functional heads and persons above that level.. Ethical standards of conduct are critical to any business and accordingly, the Employees/Officers are expected to lay down a landmark practice which may be guiding to their respective team members in their conduct and behavior. Hence, all the concerned are requested to read and understand this Code, implement the standards sought for in their day to day operations and ensure compliance with all the applicable laws, rules and regulations, this Code and all applicable policies and procedures as are adopted by the Company to govern the Conduct of its employees in any manner or form whatsoever. Nothing in this Code, in any Company's Policies and Procedures, or in other related communications (verbal or written), created or implies an employment contract or term of employment. All the employees/officers are requested to sign the acknowledgement part at the end of this Code and return the same to the Secretarial Department, indicating that they have received, read and understood and agreed to comply with the Code.
II	**HONEST AND ETHICAL CONDUCT**
	The Employees/Officers are expected to act in accordance with the highest standards of personal and professional integrity, honesty and ethical conduct while working at the Company's premises, at offsite locations where the Company's business is conducted, the company sponsored business and social events or at any other place where employees/officers are representing the Company. An honest conduct is considered to be a conduct free from fraud or deception. An ethical conduct is considered to be a conduct confirming to the accepted professional standards. An Officer should act with integrity, responsibility and in good faith. Each Officer should seek to use due care in the performance of his duties in the best interest of the Company as a whole. He should act with competence and diligence. He has an obligation, at all times, to comply with the spirit, as well as the latter, of the law and of the principles of this Code. A suggestive list of do's and don'ts for the officers is given herein below though the same is warranted to not be considered as an exhaustive one and the interpretation of the professional and ethical conduct would depend upon the circumstances of each which the Officer is expected to construe and interpret with his reasonable understanding and intelligence.

<table>
<tr><td></td><td>

For all Employees/Officer:

- Dedicate sufficient time, energy and attention to the Company to ensure diligent performance of his duties, including preparing for meetings and decision-making by reviewing in advance any materials distributed and making reasonable inquiries.
- Seek to comply with all corporate policies.
- Conduct themselves in a professionals, courteous and respectful manner.
- Comply with all applicable laws, rules and regulation/
- Act in manner to enhance and maintain the reputation of the Company.
- Respect the confidentially of information relating to the affairs of the Company acquired in the course of their services as Officers of the Company, except when authorized or legally required to disclose such information.

For Senior officers and Functional Head

- Make reasonable efforts to attend ReviewMeetings and Committee meetings regularly.
- Disclose potential conflicts of interest that they may have regarding any matters that may come before the Management, and abstain from discussion and on any matter in which the directors/officers/employees has or may have a conflict of interest.
- Make available to and share with other Colleagues information as may be appropriate to ensure proper conduct and sound operation of the Company.
- Not to use confidential information acquired in the course of their service for their personal advantage.
- A Sr Officer who has a material personal interest in any matter should notify the Management.
- The Sr Officer must bring an open and independent mind in Review/ Committee meetings and should not make a decision about any matter before attending and participating in the deliberations of the meeting.
- Act in the best interest of, and fulfill their fiduciary obligations to, Company's stakeholder.
- Where a decision in not unanimous, a dissenting Officer may disclose the fact that he dissented.

</td></tr>
<tr><td>III</td><td>

Officers are expected to dedicated their best efforts to advancing the Company's interest and to make decisions in the best interest of the company and independent of outside influences, An officer's duty demands that he avoids and disclose actual and apparent conflict of interest. A conflict of interest exists where the interest or benefits of one person or entity conflict with the interest or benefits of the Company. Examples include:

- Corporate Business Opportunities
- Acceptance of gifts / payments
- Outside employments / consultancy
- Business Interests
- Related Parties

A conflict of interest occurs when a Officer's private interest interferes in any way, or even appears to interfere, with the interest of the Company as a whole. Conflicts of interest also arise when a Officer or a member of his immediate family receives improper personal benefits as a result of his position as a Officer of the Company.

Officers shall avoid conflicts of interest with the Company. Any situation that involves, or may reasonably be expected be expected to involve, a conflict of interest with the company shall be disclosed promptly to the Management of the Company.

</td></tr>
</table>

IV	CORPORATES BUSINESS OPPORTUNITIES
	A corporate business opportunity is an opportunity • In the Company's line of business or proposed expansion or diversification, • Which the company is financially able to undertke and • Which may be of interest to the company. An officer who learns of such a corporate business opportunities and who wishes to participate in it should disclose the opportunity to the Management. If the Management determines that the company does not have an actual or expected interest in the opportunity , then, and only then, officer may participate in it, provided that the officer has not wrongfully utilized the Company's resources in order to acquire the opportunity. Officers owe a duty to the company to advance the Company's interest when the opportunity to do so arise. Officers may not ;(a) take for themselves opportunities that are discovered through the use of Company property or information or through the officer's position ; (b) use the company's property or information or the Officer's position for personal gain ; or (c) compete with the company, directly or indirectly, for business opportunities that the company is pursuing.
V	ACCEPTANCE OF GIFTS / PAYMENTS
	The officers and the members of their immediate family shall refrain themselves from accepting any offer, payments, gift or anything of value from customers, vendors, consultants or any other party etc. that is perceived a intended, directly, to However, acceptance of expensive gifts, infrequent business meals, celebratory events and entertainment, provided that they are not excessive or create an appearance of impropriety, do not violate this policy. Whenever any such valuable gifts if offered by any party, the same should be brought to the notice of the Management.
VI	COMPANY PROPERTIES
	Officers have a responsibility to safeguard and to use the company's assets and resources, as well as assets of other organizations that have been entrusted to the Company. Except as specifically authorized , assets of the Company, including equipments, materials, resources and proprietary information, must be used for company business purposes only.
VII	CONFIDENTIALITY OF INFORMATION
	Officers shall maintain the confidentiality of information entrusted to them. The Company's confidontial and proprietary information shall not be inappropriately disclosed or used for the personal gain, interest or advantage of the Officer or any one other than the Company.
VIII	FAIR DEALINGS
	Officers shall deal fairly and honestly with the company's Customers, Supliers, competitors and Employees.
XI	DISCLOSURES TO Govt AUTHORITIES AND STAKEHOLDERS
	The Company is committed to provide full fair, accurate, timely and understandable disclosure in reports and documents that are filed with or submitted to any govt authorities and other public communications. Accordingly, Company's Officers must ensure that they and other employees in the Company comply with disclosure

		controls, procedures and internal controls in financial reporting and all other Rules and Regulations as may be made applicable from time to time.
X	COMPLIANCE WITH REGULATORY FRAMWORK	
		The Officers are committed to comply with all those acts, rules regulations that govern the conduct of Company. Officers must acquire adequate knowledge of the legal requirements relating to their duties sufficient to enable them to recognize the potential dangers of violations and seek advice from the concerned department as and when necessary.
XI	ANNUAL DISCLOSURES ON COMPLAINCE WITH THE CODE	
		It shall be the duty of every officer to affirm the compliance with the code on an annual basis i.e. as on 31st March every year, such affirmation should be made within 15 days from the close of each of the financial year. In case of an officer leaving the organization at any point of time during the year, he shall give such affirmation at the time of leaving.
XII	DISCIPLINARY ACTIONS FOR VIOLATION OF THE CODE	
		Suspected violations of this Code must be reported to the CEO/Managing Director. All reported violation would be appropriately dealt with. The matters covered in this Code of Business Conduct and Ethics are of the utmost importance to the company, its stockholders and its business partners, and are essential to the Company's ability to conduct its business in accordance with its stated values. We expect all of our Officers to adhere to these rules in carrying out their duties for the Company. The Company will take appropriate action including disciplinary actions against any Employee/Officer. Disciplinary actions may include immediate termination of employment or business relationship at the Company's sole discretion. Where the company has suffered a loss, it may pursue its remedies against the individuals or entities responsible.
XIII	AMENDMENTS TO THE CODE	
		The Company is committed to continuously reviewing and updating the policies and procedures from time to time and accordingly, this Code can be modified, amended or waived of any of the provisions thereof
XIV	AKCNOWLEDGEMENT OF RECEIPT OF CODE OF ETHICS FOR ALL THE EMPLOYEES AND SR. OFFICERS	
		I have received and read the code of Conduct for the Employees and Senior Officers. I have fully understood the standards and ethics expected to be adhered and observed and I agree to comply with the same with such modifications, as may be made to it in future. If I have any questions concerning the meaning or applications of the code, any of the company's policies or the legal and regulatory requirements applicable to my post, I will consult the Management or the HR Department of the company and that my questions or reports to these sources will be maintained in confidence.

D] MARKETING STRATEGY & IMPLMENTATION PLAN

To Understand the Objectives

- Corporate Branding
- P R Exercise
- Product Marketing
- Customer Relationship

Key Features

- Short Term

  ○ To Establish Credibility of a company

- Medium Term

○ To Sell and Service Range of Products and enhance company's brand image and Customer Relationship

- Long Term

○ To create a Brand of company's product in retail segment

Product introduction

- Direct Mailing

○ Targeting the customers by acquiring database from competition or internal sources

- Advertisements

○ Print Media
○ Digital Platform

- Road Shows /Events

Medium Term Plans

- Database Building and Profiling
- Marketing and Sales Team Development
- Strengthening IT Support system
- Strengthening customer Relationship

E] MSME And Frequently Asked Questions

1 – Is MSME registration updated to Udyam Registration?

Yes, MSME registration, i.e. Udyog Aadhaar Registration has been replaced with Udyam Registration. If any micro, small and medium industries want to start any business, they can obtain the MSME/Udyam Registration. The MSME/Udyam registration is completely online. This registration provides the business with a lot of benefits and subsidies.

2 – Is the MSME registration compulsory?

No. The enterprises that come under the MSME category need not mandatorily apply for MSME registration. However, it is better to obtain MSME/Udyam registration as the government provides a lot of benefits in terms of loan facilities, easy access to credit, low-interest rates, eligibility to many schemes, etc., to the enterprises that have MSME registration.

3 – Is Aadhar card compulsory?

Yes. For obtaining Udyam registration, an Aadhaar card is compulsory. In case an applicant is other than the proprietor, the Aadhaar card of the partner and the director will be required.

4 – Can the existing and new businesses both apply?

Yes, an existing and new business can apply for MSME/Udyam Registration, provided the existing unit is functioning and meets the threshold limits for registration. Enterprises having a UAM Registration need to be re-registered for Udyam registration to avail the benefits provided for the MSMEs.

5 – *What is the validity of the MSME registration certificate?*

There is no expiry of the Udyam Registration Certificate. As long as the entity is ethical and financially healthy there will be no expiry of the certificate.

6 – *Can trading companies register under MSME?*

Yes. Earlier, the MSME registration covered only manufacturing and service industries. Trading companies are not covered by the scheme. However, in July 2021, the government announced that the wholesale and retail trade will come under the MSME classification and thus can apply for MSME registration of their wholesale/retail business. The Ministry of Micro, Small and Medium Enterprises decided to include retail and wholesale trade under MSMEs for the purpose of priority sector lending.

7 – *Do I need multiple registrations for manufacturing plants in different cities?*

No. The MSME/Udyam Registration Certificate is for a single entity irrespective of multiple branches or plants. However, information about multiple branches or plants must be furnished.

8- *Whose Aadhaar number is required to be entered when filling the MSME registration?*

In the case of a company, its authorised signatory should provide the PAN and Aadhaar number while filling the MSME registration.

9 – *Whose Aadhaar number should be entered in case a partnership firm applies for MSME registration?*

The Aadhaar number and PAN number of the proprietor is to be entered in the case of a proprietorship firm. In the case of a partnership firm, the managing partner of the firm should provide the PAN and Aadhaar number. The enterprise details on the MSME registration form will be the details of the partnership firm and the details of the entrepreneur will be the details of the managing partner in case of a partnership firm.

10 – *After registering one MSME, can I register a second MSME?*

When the enterprises are different, i.e. established under different names and registered or incorporated separately, then the proprietor of the enterprise can apply for MSME registration. However, an enterprise cannot file for more than one Udyam Registration. All the activities including manufacturing or service should be specified or added in one Udyam Registration. An entrepreneur can add additional activities in the Udyam Registration by clicking on the 'Update Details' option on the homepage.

11 – *Can a builder having a project of more than Rs.500 crore and status of business value is more than Rs.250 crore can register for MSME registration?*

No. The criteria to apply for Udyam registration depends on the annual turnover of the services provided. Since the annual business value or turnover of the builder is more than Rs.250 crore, the builder cannot apply for MSME registration as the annual turnover of an enterprise must be less than Rs.250 to apply for medium enterprise registration.

12 – *Who is eligible to apply for MSME registration?*

MSME registration can be obtained by the following entities that fulfil the revised MSME classification criteria of annual turnover and investment:

- Individuals, start-ups, business owners and entrepreneurs
- Private and public limited companies
- Sole proprietorship
- Partnership firm
- Limited Liability Partnerships (LLPs)
- Self Help Groups (SHGs)
- Co-operative societies

- Trusts

  Some important Links:
  https://www.
  F]Stay alert in Banking Transactions

- RBI Governor, bank or any such organisation does not send emails or SMS asking you to deposit money in their accounts.

- Do not respond to any emails from an unknown person offering you a huge sum of money and asking for a fee to initiate the transfer.

- Do not send any money as an initial deposit/commission/transfer fee to anyone claiming to be from RBI/Income Tax/World Bank/IMF or any such reputed organisation.

- Banks will never ask for your personal details.

- Never provide the One-Time PIN that is sent to your mobile phone to anyone.

- Always check SMS and email alerts from Banks relating to your account and report any unauthorised transactions to Your Bank immediately.